The Yellow Nib

The Yellow Nib is the annual journal of the Seamus Heaney Centre for Poetry at Queen's University Belfast. The title of the journal is inspired by a bird-call – or rather, by how that call inspired an anonymous Irish scribe of the ninth century to write the verses you see in the margin of this page. The aim of *The Yellow Nib* is simple: to publish good writing.

GENERAL EDITOR
Ciaran Carson

ADDRESS FOR CORRESPONDENCE
The Seamus Heaney Centre for Poetry
School of English
Queen's University Belfast
Belfast BT7 1NN
Northern Ireland
phone: +44 (028) 9097 1070
e-mail: shc@qub.ac.uk
www.qub.ac.uk/heaneycentre

SUBSCRIPTIONS
Gerry Hellawell
The Seamus Heaney Centre for Poetry

SUBSCRIPTION RATES
£7.00/€11 per year (Great Britain and Ireland)
€14/$18 per year (rest of the world)
All subscription rates include postage and packaging.

TRADE ORDERS AND DISTRIBUTION
Abigail Vint
Blackstaff Press
4c Heron Wharf
Sydenham Business Park
Belfast BT3 9LE
phone: +44 (028) 90455006
email: abigail.vint@blackstaffpress.com
www.blackstaffpress.com

ISSN 1745-9621
ISBN 0-85640-770-4

*Int én bec
ro léc feit
do rinn guip
   glanbuidi*

*fo-ceird faíd
ós Loch Laíg,
lon do chraíb
   charnbuidi*

9th century Irish

*The small bird
chirp-chirruped:
yellow neb,
   a note-spurt.*

*Blackbird over
Lagan water.
Clumps of yellow
   whin-burst!*

Seamus Heaney

*the little bird
that whistled shrill
from the nib of
   its yellow bill:*

*a note let go
o'er Belfast Lough—
a blackbird from
   a yellow whin*

Ciaran Carson

The
Yellow Nib

The Literary Journal of the
Seamus Heaney Centre for Poetry

VOLUME 1

2005

This volume published in 2005 by
Blackstaff Press
4c Heron Wharf, Sydenham Business Park
Belfast BT3 9LE
for The Seamus Heaney Centre for Poetry
with the assistance of the Arts Council of Northern Ireland

Printed in Irleland by Betaprint

A CIP catalogue record for this book
is available from the British Library

ISSN 1745-9621
ISBN 0-85640-770-4

www.blackstaffpress.com

Contents

Int én bec
ro léc feit
do rinn guip
    glanbuidi

fo-ceird faíd
ós Loch Laíg,
lon do chraíb
    charnbuidi

9th century Irish

The small bird
chirp-chirruped:
yellow neb,
    a note-spurt.

Blackbird over
Lagan water.
Clumps of yellow
    whin-burst!

Seamus Heaney

the little bird
that whistled shrill
from the nib of
    its yellow bill:

a note let go
o'er Belfast Lough—
a blackbird from
    a yellow whin

Ciaran Carson

Editorial

The Yellow Nib is the annual journal of the Seamus Heaney Centre
for Poetry at Queen's University Belfast. The title is inspired by a
bird-call – or rather, by how that call inspired an anonymous Irish
scribe of the ninth century to write the verses you see in the margin
of the page opposite. Perhaps, indeed, they were written by him in
the margin of a page he was working on, at the great monastery of
Bangor, on the shores of Loch Laíg, or Belfast Lough. It was the
occasional practice of Irish scribes so to divert themselves from the
copying of ecclesiastical texts. This poem looks like a typical piece of
marginalia, in its brevity and clarity, its sudden, focused attention to
the natural world. At any rate, it is cited by an an eleventh-century
metrist as an example of the syllabic verse form known as *snám súad*
– literally, 'swimming of the sages'. For all its apparent spontaneity, it
is cunningly worked.

'The Blackbird of Belfast Lough', as it is sometimes known, has
been much translated into English. The versions you see opposite are
but two possibilities. There are, to paraphrase Wallace Stevens, at
least thirteen ways of looking at a blackbird; and the blackbird can
be heard in many ways. Poetry resides in that ambiguity, and that is
why the blackbird has been chosen as the emblem of the Seamus
Heaney Centre, and its yellow beak, or neb, or nib, as the title of the
Centre's journal.

The aim of *The Yellow Nib* is simple: to publish good writing. We
hope that the contents of this first issue speak for themselves.

> I do not know which to prefer
> The beauty of inflections
> Or the beauty of innuendoes,
> The blackbird whistling
> Or just after.

Wallace Stevens, 'Thirteen Ways of Looking at a Blackbird'

CIARAN CARSON
MARCH 2005

The Blackbird of Glanmore

SEAMUS HEANEY

On the grass when I arrive,
Filling the stillness with life,
But ready to scare off
At the very first wrong move.
In the ivy when I leave.

It's you, blackbird, I love.

I park, pause, take heed.
Breathe. Just breathe and sit,
And lines I once translated
Come back: 'I want away
To the house of death, to my father,

Under the low clay roof.'

And I think of one gone to him,
A little stillness dancer –
Haunter-son, lost brother –
Cavorting through the yard,
So glad to see me home,

My homesick first term over.

The Yellow Nib, Vol. 1, 2005, pp 1–2

And I think of a neighbour's words
Long after the accident:
'Yon bird on the shed roof,
Up on the ridge for weeks –
I said nothing at the time

But I never liked yon bird.'

The automatic lock
Clunks shut, the blackbird's panic
Is shortlived, for a second
I've a bird's eye view of myself,
A shadow on raked gravel

In front of my house of life.

Hedge-hop, I am absolute
For you, your ready talkback,
Your each stand-offish comeback,
Your picky, nervy goldbeak –
On the grass when I arrive,

In the ivy when I leave.

Blackbird

JOHN WILSON FOSTER

I

The choice of the blackbird as the emblem of the Seamus Heaney
Centre for Poetry (SHCP) at Queen's University Belfast is an inspired
one. Anyone who knows Belfast and poetry knows 'The Blackbird at
Belfast Lough' ('*Int én bec*'), the anonymous haiku-like verse in Irish
from the eighth or ninth century. It is to be found translated by the
Centre's director, Ciaran Carson, and offered on the Centre's website
in both Irish and English as lyrical marginalia in the manner of
ancient manuscripts, but it is familiar too in the translations of
Seamus Heaney, John Montague and Frank O'Connor, among many
others. Hurlstone Jackson in *A Celtic Miscellany* (1951) calls it an
epigram, not in the Wildean sense but in the sense of a brief poem
on a single subject that achieves maximum compression and force.

The diversity of the translations and the formal nature of the
verse, competing (it seems to me) with the mundane if lyrical subject
of a common bird warbling from a bush, is the very emblem of the
rich ambiguity of poetry to which Ciaran Carson refers in his
introduction to the Centre on its website. The poem has had an
alluring quality for Irish poets. Translating it seems almost a kind of
obligatory exercise of the kind engaged in by aspiring musicians or,
one imagines, apprentice bards in the century in which it was
composed. But it is easy to fancy the tantalisingly short poem
mischievously welcoming translations of itself, while actually daring
Irish poets to achieve the definitive version; its brevity is the
enticement and the deception. And this too seems emblematic of the

The Yellow Nib, Vol. 1, 2005, pp 3–11
© John Wilson Foster

welcome the SHCP will extend to poets far and wide, a welcome not
untinged with challenge. Yes, indeed, an inspired logo and epigraph
for the Centre.

Like Ezra Pound's sudden petals on a wet black bough, the poem's
blackbird has the immediacy of apparition. This conjuring of small
miracle out of the everyday of nature requires an incongruity, like
Patrick Kavanagh's bluebells in a throughother landscape. The
blackbird (*Turdus merula merula* L.) is an everyday of nature, resident
with us all year round, though larger numbers come in and out of
Britain and Ireland in spring and autumn, and is the fourth most
common bird among us, up to ten million pairs strong. It is also an
everywhere of nature, observable throughout our mainlands and
islands and facing the stern task of living in woodlands, gardens,
town parks, uplands, thickets, rocky coasts and virtually treeless
islands. In 1849 William Thompson (in *The Natural History of
Ireland*) described blackbirds as common and resident throughout
Ireland; 'they likewise resort to the islands off the coasts.' Thompson
is never bare of anecdotes about the species he describes, and he
notes that when the severe Ulster winter of 1813–14 began to relent,
over a hundred blackbirds and thrushes were found floating dead on
the stream flowing from a spring at Ballynafeigh, near Belfast, a
stream presumably long buried by bricks and stones.

Yet the familiarity of this abundant bird has never bred our
contempt, unlike in the house sparrow's case, a contempt we now
regret as the sparrow dwindles in numbers and deserts our eaves, its
chirrupings falling silent. For the blackbird has combined abundance
with caution, even hauteur. William Yarrell in 1843 (in *A History of
British Birds*) saw the blackbird as 'shy, restless, and vigilant' while
W.H. Hudson in 1895 (in *British Birds*) saw it as a skulker, ready to
take alarm and flight in a trice, uttering its irritated chatter. Habits
change, of course: in my boyhood I had to reach the countryside from
Belfast before I saw the wary hooded crow; now it is brazen and has
penetrated the city. And there were magpies in suburban Dublin
gardens but not in Belfast gardens; now they too are everywhere and
may have helped drive the sparrow into decline. But the blackbird
has not changed his ways much; he is still the neighbourhood watch
and still utters his exasperating tic-tic from the bushes at twilight (as

does the American robin), as if bedding the other species down like some scolding night nurse, then he's up again at dawn or earlier and rousing his fellows. He will not ingratiate himself with us like the European robin and maintains his distance and dignity, and this makes him a fitter subject for the detachment of 'The Blackbird at Belfast Lough'. I say 'he', and in doing so I note Frank Finn's comment in 1900 (in *Birds of our Country*) that for some reason or other hens of the blackbird species are seen far less often than cocks. This is fortuitous (the hen being the twitcher's medium-sized brown job) but odd. Is it that the cock is simply seen more often because of the contrast with his backdrop? Back in British Columbia, I see seven or eight female northern harriers (what are known here as hen harriers) to one male – which is not fortuitous, since the male is a more splendid creature than his mate – and have no idea why.

It is the cock blackbird's darkness that sets off the almost startling brightness of his bill – easy to see how he surprised the medieval poet with beauty. Alfred Lord Tennyson in 'The Blackbird' imagined the 'gold dagger' of the bird's bill. In the Belfast poem, the yellow bill echoes the yellow of the gorse. John Montague called the Belfast blackbird 'yoke-billed'. Yet Witherby *et al.* in the once biblical *Handbook of British Birds* (1938) describe the bill as orange and so too does Ludwig Koch in his *Encyclopedia of British Birds* (1955). Yarrell chooses gamboge, the yellow pigment derived from the gum resin, and other writers too opt for yellow. But then Witherby *et al.* describe the cock's plumage as glossy and so too do Koch and T.A. Coward (in *The Birds of the British Isles*, 1950), but though they are experts they are wrong. The starling is glossy but not the blackbird. Finn rightly notes the lack of metallic reflections in the feathers, and I would describe the feathering as more matt than glossy. In any case, the colour lies in the bird's name, which the poet economically uses to achieve the black–yellow contrast in his vision of the bird. By the way, Carson's description of the bill as a nib is not just an agreeable piece of licence that neatly appropriates the bird and the poem for the institutional task he has set them. Nib originally meant beak or nose and is related etymologically to neb: neb is the word Heaney uses in his translation ('yellow neb'), and neb meant not just the nose, as I thought ('Don't stick your neb in!'), but a bird's beak. So the bird's whistle is a poet's song, neb is nib, and poets are now encouraged to sing in the vicinity of Belfast Lough as of old.

Carson sees the Belfast blackbird's song as a note let go, Heaney as a 'note-spurt', Frank O'Connor as a cry tossed over Belfast Lough. It is as though the original poet has frozen the song in one frame, for the joy of the blackbird's song is its continuity, which it shares with the more plangent song of the robin and the nightingale (though I haven't been fortunate enough to hear the latter). The song thrush starts and stops, repeats once, twice or even three times (Browning, in 'Home Thoughts from Abroad', settled for once), but the blackbird launches into lovely arias in a voice fuller-bodied than any other songbird I've heard. Flute-like is the frequent epithet. Everyone agrees on the disappointing falling off at song's end, but the ease of delivery the *Handbook of British Birds* refers to is at one with this and stands in contrast to the beautiful but, as it were, self-conscious effort of the song thrush, trying again to get it right the next time. Richard Jefferies (quoted by Hudson) thought the blackbird sings 'in a quiet, leisurely way, as a great master should'. So cool is the blackbird that he has been known to sing on the wing, and in Derry this spring I heard him carry on his song as he floated and swooped from one rooftop to another a hundred yards off, not bothering to interrupt his aria. His is the finest song I know and the one I'd take to the proverbial desert island, though the song I'd want to hear at journey's end would be the brief spiralling diminuendo of a Swainson's thrush that truly echoes like day's epitaph in the forests of British Columbia.

However, we are no longer connoisseurs of birdsong because we are no longer bird fanciers. Revd C.A. Johns in *British Birds in their Haunts* (1909) quotes Johann Bechstein (1757–1822) on the noisy nature of the blackbird's song and its unsuitability for the cage. Yarrell also remarked without irony that the blackbird's song is much too loud 'except for the open air'! Ours until the mid-twentieth century was a culture of cage-birds, in which linnets, mules (canary–linnet crosses), song thrushes, blackbirds and robins were prized for their song. There are entries in Samuel Pepys's diary for May 1663 about a blackbird a house carpenter had sent him and for which the carpenter had been offered twenty shillings, 'for he do so whistle', and which indeed warbled well except Pepys complained it started 'many tunes' and then left them and went no further. I like to think the blackbird was too wayward a fellow to be well caged.

II

Surely the yellow bill and sweet song prevented the blackbird from the malign associations of blackness we find in the pre-Christian Irish sagas and other surviving folklores and which invest the hapless cormorants and crows. In his entry for the blackbird, John J. Watters in his *Natural History of the Birds of Ireland* (1853) quotes the Sunnah (the body of traditional sayings supplementing the Koran), but perhaps the following need not blacken the name of our familiar bird: 'the souls of those in Purgatory were in the crops of blackbirds, exposed to hell fire morning and evening, until the Judgement Day.' It is true that in the Early Christian voyage tales in Ireland, tortured souls in the shapes of birds are encountered frequently. By contrast, in the medieval Irish stories and poems, there are expressions of what the Belfast scholar Helen Waddell called 'mutual charities between saints and beasts' (1934). Birdsong, because it is intelligible to us (though we don't hear the challenge and threat that song is often meant to mount), surely encourages mutual charity. One of the most delightful stories Waddell reproduces concerns St Kevin (d. Glendalough, AD 618), whose hand outstretched to heaven during a Lenten contemplation was chosen by a blackbird for her nest. The bird laid eggs and hatched young before the saint would bring himself to move. St Kevin has stretched his arm through the window of his hut, for the bird's truest habitat is outdoors while the saint's is indoors. Jackson (*Celtic Miscellany*) reproduces an epigram from the eleventh or twelfth century, 'The Hermit Blackbird', which seems to voice the holy man's envy of the bird's life without obligation, even though he sees both of them as hermits:

> Ah, blackbird, it is well for you where your nest is in the bushes;
> a hermit that clangs no bell, sweet, soft and peaceful is your call.

The relative solitariness of the blackbird allowed the poetic monk to see the bird as a reclusive anchorite like himself. He presumably did not see parties of blackbirds on migration or in roosts. In the 1950s I saw dozens of blackbirds each evening cross the old Hillfoot Road (the future ring road) on the south side of Belfast city, flying from the hilly hedgerows to a communal roost in the city that I was never able to locate.

In Austin Clarke's version of an eighteenth-century lay, 'The Blackbird of Derrycairn' ('Lon Doire an Chairn'), it is the blackbird rather than the holy man who is speaking. The bird recalls Fionn's discovery of the blackbird in Norway and his return to Ireland with it 'to gild the branch and tell, there, / Why men must welcome in the daylight'. Above all the sounds of the country, Fionn prized 'My throat rejoicing from the hawthorn'. The bird is speaking to a monk (perhaps a novice) and reminds him that 'no handbell gives a glad sound', while knowledge is found not in the monastery but 'among the branches', an idea of the roofless school (later adopted by William Wordsworth): 'Listen! That song that shakes my feathers / Will thong the leather of your satchels.' The blackbird seems to have played its pagan role in the contest between the elder faiths of Ireland and imported medieval Christianity.

Clarke's translation is said to have been an oblique criticism of the theocracy of Free State Ireland and the original to have been a Jacobite lay, and if the latter is the case, the bird played a rebel part. In an anonymous eighteenth-century broadside entitled 'The Royal Blackbird', the bird is the Old Pretender, the son of James II. The speaker fears that a fowler has taken his blackbird, which once flourished in England and is a stranger there now, though respected in Scotland as well as in France and Spain. The broadside exploits a kind of eco-politics: it deals with rarity and extinction, over-zealous hunting and adaptation – names of appropriate countries are inserted according to where the ballad was recited or printed. It first appeared around 1715 but was still popular in the nineteenth century, according to Georges-Denis Zimmermann, who reminds us (in *Songs of Irish Rebellion*, 1967) that Patrick Dinneen in his famous Irish–English dictionary translated *londubh* as 'a blackbird; a Jacobite, a rapparee, a hero'.

A curious feature of Irish nationalist culture in the eighteenth and nineteenth centuries is the way natural elements or species were invested with political symbolism. Irish nature was recruited in order to advance the cause: in 'The Croppy Boy', for instance, the sweetly singing birds change their notes from tree to tree, 'and the song they sang was "Old Ireland free"'. Birds and animals could help disguise political protest and conspiracy. The blackbird, dark-robed, singular, whistling with deceptive innocence, often skulking and fleeing, was a natural for the part.

The title of one broadside from the Year of Revolutions, 1848, 'Granua's Lament for the Loss of her Blackbird Mitchel, the Irish Patriot', identifies the latest role assigned to the bird. The ballad is full of the circumstances of the Fenian John Mitchel's arrest for sedition and deportation and there is little extension to the metaphor of the bird itself.

New words were set to the air of 'The Royal Blackbird' in 1881 and turned Charles Stewart Parnell into 'The Blackbird of Avondale'. Here is a female Ireland who laments Parnell's imprisonment, as she lamented Mitchel's banishment, and as in the Jacobite ballad, it is a base fowler who captures and carries off the bird. Apart from the obvious political circumstances there is also an implied story and cultural context involving a beautiful woman who has a pet blackbird that sweetly sings but that is snared by a trapper presumably netting or 'liming' songsters for the cage, a common professional and amateur occupation until the early twentieth century. In the blackbird's absence, it is the linnet and thrush who must warble, but with their sadder notes.

Since the speaker of 'The Blackbird of Avondale' is expressly unconsoled by the song of the nightingale (which is absent from Ireland for natural reasons), either the broadside was distributed in England as well as Ireland, or the birds are simply generic presences. Certainly the blackbird became an adaptable figure detached from real nature. The traditional Irish song 'If I Was a Blackbird' reduces the bird to a mere figure of flight; in this secular rather than political love song, the lovelorn speaker simply wishes for the power of flight so that she might follow the ship in which her sweetheart sails in search of fortune; under the circumstances she would have been better off wishing to be, say, a blackheaded gull. But in the song the

landlocked lover would, as a blackbird, build her nest in the ship's
rigging. One can almost imagine a real blackbird doing the same,
fond as she is of odd choices of location for her nest, and migrating
perching birds do sometimes make landfall on a moving ship and stay
for a while. Older readers may remember the hit that whistling
Ronnie Ronalde made of this song in the 1950s, the verb in its title
subjunctivised. No more real, ornithologically speaking, is the bird in
the even more famous and curiously moving 'Bye Bye Blackbird',
composed in 1926 by Ray Henderson and Mort Dixon. This is an
American Tin Pan Alley song and since none of the various
American blackbirds are songsters, the composers have a bird in
mind as fictional as Vera Lynn's bluebirds that were to fly over
Dover's white cliffs. Unless Henderson and Dixon, when they write
of the blackbird singing the blues all day outside the speaker's door,
are thinking of the curious bluesy warble of the red-winged blackbird.
(And we could argue that Lynn's bluebirds are familiar legendary
embodiments of happiness that will appear when the tide of war
turns against Hitler and in favour of Britain.)

The base fowler makes a comeback in one of the few poems by
Francis Ledwidge to gain fame – 'The Blackbirds', which Padraic
Colum retitled 'Lament for the Poets: 1916' for an anthology. In a
natural progression, the mourning young maiden of 'The Blackbird
of Avondale' has become the keening old woman of Irish sorrows,
the Shan Van Vocht (or Poor Old Woman), who mourns the capture
of her blackbird by the fowler at dawn and who grieves 'the silent
bills', in this case the silencing of Patrick Pearse, Thomas
MacDonagh and Joseph Plunkett, who were executed for their part
in the Easter Rising. During that tragic week in 1916, Ledwidge was
otherwise engaged in the service of the British Crown in the First
World War, though, like many of the Irish volunteers, he saw himself
as fighting for Ireland as much as for Britain. When the Old Woman
predicts that the skylarks will dip their wings when they fly over the
graves of the martyrs, we have an image that suggests the gesture of
respect made by aeroplanes, which Ledwidge would have seen in
action in the skies above Europe. And in future dawns, blackbirds
will appear, singing with love of the executed.

Ledwidge wrote several poems about the blackbird, one entitled

'To an Irish Blackbird at Dawn', in which 'yella bill' sings in gladness to mark the refusal of grief by the speaker, either an Irish small farmer mourning a lost child, or a woman of the countryside mourning a sweetheart who died young. Patrick MacGill, also an Irish volunteer in British uniform, recalled in his memoir *The Red Horizon* (1915) one dawn in the trenches when 'a blackbird hopped on to the parapet, looked inquiringly in, his yellow bill moving from side to side, and fluttered away', and a skylark rising and falling, nature's life mocking mankind's death, but also offering the consoling and encouraging idea that life goes on despite the trenches, and will go on after them.

The blackbird is a bird for all seasons, and the Seamus Heaney Centre has done well to recruit his potent reality and equally potent symbolism.

Three Poems

JORGE LUIS BORGES

Translated from the Spanish by Norman Thomas di Giovanni

Sleep

Night sets on us its magic task:
to ravel out the world, the endless branchings
of cause and effect, which lose themselves in time's
unfathomed vertigo. Night demands that every night
you forget your name, your blood, and those who bore you,
each human word, each tear, and everything
that being awake has ever taught you – geometry's
imaginary point, the line, the plane, the cube,
the pyramid, the cylinder, the sea and waves,
the coolness of clean sheets, gardens, empires,
the Caesars, Shakespeare, and, what's hardest of all,
the one you love. Strange to think that a pill,
blotting the cosmos out, lets chaos in.

The Yellow Nib, Vol. 1, 2005, pp 12–14

A Dream

In an out-of-the-way corner of Iran rises a stone tower, doorless, windowless, not very tall. In its one room, whose walls form a circle and whose floor is beaten earth, stand a wooden table and a bench. And in this circular cell a man who looks like me is writing, in characters I cannot understand, a long poem about a man in another circular cell writing a poem about a man in yet another circular cell. The series has no end, nor will anyone ever read what these prisoners are writing.

On Forgetting a Dream
To Viviana Aguilar

In the ambiguous dawn I had a dream.
I know that in the dream were many doors.
The rest I've lost. This morning,
as I woke, the intimate fable
fell away and became as shadowy
as Ur of the Chaldees,
the darkness of Tiresias,
or the corollaries of Spinoza.
I have spent my life deciphering
the dogmas that philosophers uphold.
As everyone knows, an Irishman once said
that God's attention, which never sleeps,
perceives for ever every dream,
each tear, each solitary garden.
Uncertainty lingers, the darkness spreads.
If I knew what became of that dream
I dreamt – or that I dream I dreamt –
then I would know all things.

TRANSLATOR'S NOTE

Jorge Luis Borges, the Argentine poet and writer, wielded enormous influence
on world literature during the last half of the twentieth century. He died in 1986.
The poems 'Sueño', 'Un sueño', and 'Al olvidar un sueño' are from *La Cifra* (1981).

Eerts

MARCIAL SOUTO

Translated from the Spanish by Norman Thomas di Giovanni

Anselm Curtis took one last look at the eerts, then turned away and went indoors.

'Clara, there it goes again,' he said, vexed. 'Just like yesterday. The same quaking, banging. I don't know what's going on.'

'Not again!' Clara said. 'That explains why all our cups and saucers are jiggling.'

That autumn, when they first arrived and moved into the end house in the close, Anselm and Clara Curtis found their back garden a mass of spindly trees that branched out in a tangle of fibrous shoots.

These branches made them think more of a ball of roots than of a tree, and when spring came the Curtises had their earliest inkling that there was something odd about these plants. No leaves or flowers filled them out. The twigs swelled a bit but then turned brittle. And all the while the branches – if that's what they were – gave the impression that they were really roots.

'Anselm,' Clara had one day said, 'I've been thinking. Maybe whoever set out these trees made a mistake and planted the seedlings upside down. Maybe their roots are sprouting, while their crowns lie buried in the soil.'

In time, Clara and Anselm got used to the trees and, as a joke, called them *eerts*, for it was plain that their garden was filled with plants that were growing the wrong way round.

Of course, the Curtises breathed no word of this to anyone. Beyond their garden fence, in a stretch of open fields, eerts grew out of control. They were of all shapes and sizes, but the nearest were somewhat taller. How strange, thought Clara and Anselm, that none of the neighbours showed any interest in them.

The Curtises had tried to graft the eerts in their garden with slips of apple and pear trees, but their efforts came to naught. The slips soon wilted and died. It was clear that all the plants were good for was firewood.

'Yes, they're queer all right,' said the butcher, who lived next door. 'I still remember when they first appeared. That was twenty years ago. Now they're everywhere. I've heard there's a whole wood of them across the river.'

'Clara,' said Anselm Curtis one night after he and his wife had gone to bed, 'I'm worried about these trees. Can you picture a whole wood, roots in the air and trunks, branches and leaves buried in the ground?'

The very next morning, a warm summer's day, the Curtises were sitting out in their back garden looking at the brownish tangle of eerts.

'Yes, Clara, they must be roots,' Anselm said.

Just then there came a slow *thud, thud*, and the earth shivered.

'See, it's started again,' he said.

The shaking and shuddering went on for nearly an hour. The ground wobbled. The plants trembled.

'They must be the roots of full-grown trees,' Anselm went on. 'They're thick and bushy. And this feeling that there's no air to breathe. Are they taking oxygen and carrying it to their branches instead of making it for us? Can that be how they get their nourishment? Can their leaves and branches really grow down into the earth? Who do you suppose planted them – and why?'

'None of that matters,' said Clara. 'They're just plants and they grow whichever way they like.'

'But that *whack, whack*ing. It only comes from the eerts. It has to be connected with them. This must be their growing season.'

'I don't think so, Anselm.'

'What can it be, then? Listen. Are they hitting bedrock? Are their trunks splintering because they can't spread any other way? What else do you think can be going on?'

Clara sighed and suddenly gasped, trying hard to fill her lungs. Then she held a hand up to her mouth.

'Someone's chopping them down,' she heard herself say.

The upside-down tree
© Miriam de Burca

TRANSLATOR'S NOTE

Marcial Souto, author, translator, and editor, was born in Spain and grew up in Montevideo and Buenos Aires. His books include *Para bajar a un pozo de estrellas* (1983) and *Trampas para pesadillas* (1988). 'Lobras' ('Eerts') is from the former collection.

Saturday Morning

ALAN GILLIS

The fart and snigger of sausages and free-
range eggs, the beans of a coffee grinder,
and light house music on a Fujifilm CD
blank out of mind the mortuary white
yellow shake of your hands, the humming
tube of your kitchen's fluorescent light.

Hitachi diggers stack mud, roots and scree
into mountains, then abandon them to
slouch indifferently over traffic heard
charging from the city like buffalo,
stampeding towards Burger Kings in the country,
family estrangements, malls of born-again logos.

Foamy-chopped dogs frisk the pavements
for barf-free kebab, or hot dropped fry,
mobiles trilling de-daw-de-dee theme tunes,
their birdsong jukeboxing the cigarette air,
as rain falls from a plum sky on taxis
hunting for knickered, knackered, come-down fares.

You sing a little, the music and pork fingers
oozing through you until backwashed in blue
half-slips, red halternecks and voluptuary
ankle braids, the armpits of the night
criss-crossed in car parks and harbours,
your thub-a-dub-dub turned ting-a-ling-ding.

The Yellow Nib, Vol. 1, 2005, pp 18–21

You slob on the sofa's shucking leather:
advice on contemporary interiors
hmms from a tube-lit screen, as you raft
into waterdark, your parts equidistant,
tacked with Pritt Stick, or with UHU glue –
the you who is there, and the you who isn't.

You are happy when the room disappears,
when the dull glass drizzles into static
then flicks to the colours of *Columbo*
or *The World*, and you pow-wow with live stars
and interact with football or violent nature
shows, as models hootchy-kootchy on blue guitars.

In open fields, unleashed and hairy men belt
leather balls with bootlaces, mouths foaming,
dribbling and colliding under a throne
of purple fire, riotous in jockstraps
below on-gushing winds. By covered rivers
they are casting flies, watching the ripple-laps.

In pools they dunk into public water,
kow-towing to children hung off their necks,
while you ooze through your own dibble-dapple
letting thought-bubbles lather your head,
lolling into the whirlpools of their suds,
skimming the fronds of your ink-dark riverbed.

Where a river-grey tsunami hammer-
walled through the coastal village, an orange
Clio is perched on a green Wych Elm.
Click. On arctic chops, a black and mammoth
keel welts into a beluga, its blood
staining the floes like sweet vermouth.

Click. A celebrity chef provides fresh ideas
for sausages. Click. The merlin falls like a brick

on a bank vole's head. Click. The President.
Click. The pop star peels down to his gonads.
Click. 'Oh my God, look at her kitchen!' Click.
Janjaweed teenagers patrol the road to Chad.

A band plays Down. Outside the Green
Party members blank out the erotics of cars
the colour of tiger lilies, while a tweety
bird jacuzzis among the anklets and pâtéd
burgers of a gutter-stream. It's a perfect day
to draw the blinds and blow your mind away.

Outside the wind shushes the shivering trees,
rising with the whine of a worried hairdryer
into the bow-wow whooshing of a sonic jet-stream
overhead, as a plane flickers on the canvas
of overwhelming blue, stringing its vapour trails
to Ho Chi Minh City, or the green plains of Kansas.

If you lie there long enough you'll grow roots
deep in the sofa's core, your face swarming
into pixels, a hodgepodge of static
sucked into thin air, or gobbled by worms
of underground cable, to be spewed out
on a screen in the office of an advertising firm.

Lie there long enough and you will drown
in the glut-stream of yourself, or nothing,
as you dissolve into the screen, its thin lips
gaping into such a maw, you cannot undo
its babbling hoodoo. Lie back long enough
in your caramel dream and the sky will spew

down leatherwood trees and blue slate,
scudding waves rising, the gobbledegook
wind no longer passing, plates colliding,
green plains pooled, as children in nylon clothing

splish-splash and wade through a dreamtime
torrent of footballs, joysticks, teacups flowing

along the flushing terraced street,
until hauled by their parents onto rooftops
to feed the ducks by chimneypots.
'Brush both sides so it doesn't stick.'
Click. The President. Click. 'And the lucky
winner is.' Click. 'I've always loved you.' Click.

'The future is Orange.' The gas fire of the sun
will raze the savannahs that remain,
their open fields swollen like a torture victim's
viced tongue, pulled out and fag-burnt and blistered
into bubblewrap, red ants dancing on bone piles
sprawled as if the skeletons were playing twister.

Last night's pilau rice flickers through your blue
carpet, wormy grains writhing in a candescent
masala, dancing on the dead white plate,
as you get up to take a leak, survey
the cleaning heavens, the children kicking ball,
and open your inclusive guide to Saturday.

Outside pensioners slouch towards hospital
wards and their partners, or blank rooms without
partners, as the men return, refreshed from
their combat. And with a stained yellow finger
you flick on *Deep Rider*, in which the hero, Randy,
hump-humps his American humdinger

in blue car parks and harbours, his pallid
cheeks lit by water-light. And blank out of mind
the hum rising behind the flickering glass,
hissing and sniggering through the crevasse
of your smug and peeling sofa's leather.
A new show's beginning. Pull yourself together.

Philip Larkin and
Belfast Literary Culture

Based on a paper delivered at the conference
'Queen's Thinkers: The Intellectual Heritage of a University'
3 April 2004

EDNA LONGLEY

At a book launch in the Bookshop at Queen's an English novelist remarked: 'Surely that's not Philip Larkin up there!' He was puzzled by Larkin's presence on the bookshop's frieze among such Irish literary worthies as J.M. Synge and Medbh McGuckian. Equally, what has Larkin to do with Belfast literary culture beyond the fact that he was sub-librarian at Queen's from 1950 to 1955, in a misty Belfast which knew nothing of book launches, and wrote some poems here? Indeed, 'Philip Larkin and Belfast Literary Culture' is a title I was given for the 'Queen's Thinkers' conference rather than one I chose. Yet the problems raised by 'Philip Larkin and Belfast Literary Culture' may be more intriguing than an obvious topic like 'John Hewitt and Belfast Literary Culture'.

To start with three problems. First, Larkin didn't think of himself as a 'thinker' let alone a Queen's one. He moaned in November 1951 'This time next week ... I'm featured in a *Brains Trust* at the English Society. Holy God! ... I suppose I'm there to provide comic relief' (SL, 177). More seriously, when interviewed by Anthony Thwaite about his *Oxford Book of Twentieth-Century English Verse* (1973), Larkin thus excused his failure to write a preface: 'I'm not a theorist, I'm not a critic, I'm not an academic' (FR, 102). And in a later interview: 'I've never had "ideas" about poetry' (RW, 76). In fact,

Larkin saw the rise of university criticism as corrupting literature. Writing to Thwaite in 1974 he satirised the poet-academic Donald Davie to the tune of 'Daisy, daisy':

> Davie, Davie,
> Give me a bad review;
> That's your gravy,
> Telling chaps what to do.
> Forget about sense and passion
> As long as it's in the fashion –
> But let's be fair,
> It's got you a chair,
> And a billet in Frogland too. (SL, 501–2)

Davie was then a professor at Stanford University, California, and had a house in France.

Second, aside from his closeness to Kingsley Amis, Larkin was a literary loner. He was neither coterie material nor one of those messianic poets like Yeats who need cohorts, disciples, a creative community, a cultural revival, a national revolution, global apocalypse. He might contribute to the local BBC radio programme *The Arts in Ulster*, or review for the Queen's magazine *Q*, but he insisted on solitude as the essential condition of the lyric poet, the essential condition for writing lyric poetry. A poem from 1951, 'Best Society', shows the poet retreating to his upstairs rooms in the now-vanished 30 Elmwood Avenue. The poem dramatises a recurrent position in Larkin's poetry: the artist's necessary refusal of the social world:

> Viciously, then, I lock my door.
> The gas-fire breathes. The wind outside
> Ushers in evening rain. Once more
> Uncontradicting solitude
> Supports me on its giant palm;
> And like a sea-anemone
> Or simple snail, there cautiously
> Unfolds, emerges, what I am.

This is a portrait of Larkin doing his kind of thinking. Later, his Belfast retrospects would nostalgically evoke the cloistered space of evenings devoted to the Muse.

Third, 'Belfast Literary Culture' not only implies writers hanging out, but a kind of localism or regionalism that Larkin never embraced. He and Amis are often attached by critics, if problematically again, to the 1950s non-metropolitan formation dubbed simply 'the Movement'. But these writers' horizon was provincial (an English provincialism) rather than regional. They assumed a provincial-metropolitan rather than regional-cosmopolitan literary axis. To quote from Blake Morrison's *The Movement* (1980): 'This provincialism is not to be confused with "regionalism", a mode of writing which the Movement saw as consisting of a sentimental and usually Celtic celebration of one's roots.' Hewitt's Ulster regionalism is a case in point: his belief that a writer must be 'a rooted man'. Larkin and Hewitt coincided in Belfast but they made no literary common cause. When Amis won the 1955 Somerset Maugham Award (which required the recipient to travel), Larkin noted that a travel book by Amis was about as likely as 'a space-thriller by John Hewitt' (SL, 244). A regionalist manifesto by Philip Larkin would have been unlikely too. For Larkin and Amis, the literary cult of Abroad and the literary cult of roots were equally objectionable. In 1967, after a decade in Hull, Larkin joked: 'I am not even turning into a regional poet, with his clay pipe and acknowledged corner in the snug of the Cat and Fuddle' (SL, 393). He introduced Douglas Dunn's anthology *A Rumoured City: New Poets from Hull* (1982) by saying just that Hull is 'as good a place to write as any'. Larkin's Hull, like his Belfast, primarily constitutes a neutral cloister for the Muse's visitations, for 'uncontradicting solitude'. He goes on to call Hull 'a city that is in the world, yet sufficiently on the edge of it to have a different resonance. Behind Hull is the plain of Holderness, lonelier and lonelier ...' (FR, 128).

Now to reverse everything said so far. Larkin is, after all, a poet of subtle masks and dialectics, not to mention jokes, ironies and teases. His refusals affirm principles. First, Larkin is a hugely important thinker *about* poetry as well as in it. Second, Belfast influenced his poetry. Third, he influenced the poets who, in the 1960s, would be viewed collectively as 'Belfast poets'. Overall, Larkin's time here can be seen as a key moment in the complex interactions that continue to shape modern poetry in these islands.

On my first point: Larkin's contribution to the aesthetics of modern poetry is both considerable and underrated. Even if he wrote no systematic *ars poetica*, he left a significant body of criticism – reviews, interviews, the writings about jazz which are disguised poetry criticism. And when Larkin disavows theory, he is really questioning other poets' theories. Here his main butt is the 'modernism' of T.S. Eliot and Ezra Pound, or more strictly its academic exegesis. In 1964 Larkin complained to Ian Hamilton that 'poetry seems to have got into the hands of a critical industry which is concerned with culture in the abstract, and this I ... lay at the door of Eliot and Pound' (FR, 19). By 'culture in the abstract' – as opposed to culture freshly lived – Larkin means the literariness of modernism: all those quotations in Eliot's *Waste Land* and Pound's *Cantos*. In a broadcast of 1958 he called poetry 'a skill easily damaged by self-consciousness' (FR 78). Since self-consciousness infects content as much as style, he also doubted a poet's duty to be topical. In 1957, contributing to a *London Magazine* symposium on 'The Writer in His Age', he said: 'A man may believe that what we want at present is a swingeing good novel on the state of this or the fate of that, but his imagination remains unstirred except by notions of renunciation or the smell of a certain brand of soap' (FR, 4). Thus Larkin challenged an increase in poetic self-consciousness for which he mainly blamed the academy. And he distrusted critical and political fashions that 'tell poets what to do', to apply his Davie lampoon. All this indicates that Larkin's own 'idea' of poetry is extremely pure. It combines an aroma of *fin de siècle* aestheticism with a central tenet of Romanticism: the primacy of inspiration. Poetry depends on what 'stirs' the imagination. In 1957 again, he insisted: 'writing a poem is ... not an act of the will ... Whatever makes a poem successful is not an act of the will' (RW, 84). The distinctiveness of Larkin's imaginative world derives from its truth to his stirrings and feelings – however dark some of these may be.

Biographical revelations about Larkin have at least corrected the false impression that he is a social-realist poet rather than a

Romantic aesthete who explores disturbing psychic zones. Similarly, his formal achievement is now properly recognised. Larkin was more steeped in literature, more profoundly allusive, than he pretended. His hostility to the Eliot–Pound hegemony (although his poetic taste was much more eclectic than some suppose) signifies commitment to what Yeats calls 'those traditional metres that have developed with the language'. In one interview Larkin sums up 'writing poetry' in Yeatsian terms as 'playing off the natural rhythms and word order of speech against the artificialities of rhyme and metre', and describes what he learned from Yeats and Auden as 'the management of lines, the formal distancing of emotion' (RW, 71, 67). Larkin completed all his creative apprenticeships during his Belfast years. He wrote three-quarters of *The Less Deceived* (1955) in the city, and the first poem in the collection, 'Lines on a Young Lady's Photograph Album', at once *ars poetica* and love poem, consummates what has happened to his inner landscape: 'What grace / Your candour thus confers upon her face! / How overwhelmingly persuades / That this is a real girl in a real place // In every sense empirically true'. This apostrophe to photography defines Larkin's aesthetic as an empirical openness to sensation that engenders new kinds of reality. At the same time, his 'real' and 'true' are not limited to the material plane or to the album's implicitly Northern Irish scenes: they aspire to the condition of symbol.

At another level (to move on to my second point) the poem proves that Larkin got out more in Belfast than his self-images imply. Later in the evening he would leave the cloister, drink, play bridge, listen to jazz. The smaller, more collegiate, less managerial Queen's of that day gave him a busy social life and two intense amours. The 'real girl in a real place' was Winifred Arnott, a graduate of the English Department, then working in the Library. And, insofar as she is the Muse of *The Less Deceived*, perhaps her real place obliquely lights the poems as does the real girl's symbolic translation. Larkin finally says of the Hull anthology: 'These poems are not about Hull, yet it is unseen in all of them, the permission of a town that lets you write' (FR, 128).

A hint of how Belfast affected Larkin's aesthetic lies in his phrase 'the formal distancing of emotion'. Belfast, as well as form, gave his poetry distance or perspective. Larkin's sexual liaisons and their poetic fallout were eased by distance from his family and relationships in England. A poem about 'Arrival' in Belfast hails a newness (whose 'ignorance of me / Seems a kind of innocence') that buries the past. He christens the city, improbably, a 'milk-aired Eden' (CP, 51). As with Larkin's personal past, so with his English cultural affiliations. Just after returning to England he wrote 'The Importance of Elsewhere' (1955): a poem about the enabling effects of distance and difference, the disabling effects of closeness:

> Lonely in Ireland, since it was not home,
> Strangeness made sense. The salt rebuff of speech,
> Insisting so on difference, made me welcome:
> Once that was recognised, we were in touch ... (CP, 104)

Here Belfast's exoticism, its different language – not just voice – is recalled as liberating. Later, the poem says of England: 'These are my customs and establishments / It would be much more serious to refuse. / Here no elsewhere underwrites my existence.' This is another *ars poetica*. In Ireland Larkin felt less spiritually (not politically) coerced by English 'customs and establishments'. He felt freer to explore both his own 'strangeness' and an England which Ireland's strangeness brought into focus. 'Church-Going' (CP, 97), often seen as a quintessentially 'English' poem, was sparked off in 1954 by a Northern Irish church. Yet, despite the ineradicable reflex whereby he 'thrilled to the accent of that sharp skylined city' (SL, 393), Larkin was wary of either going native in Belfast or becoming a professional expat. His memoir of 'The Library I Came to' (*Gown Literary Supplement*, 1984) concludes: 'I was sorry to go, but I had been at Queen's nearly five years, and I could not see myself as an Anglo-Ulsterman with a cottage at Cushendall and an adopted accent.'

Finally, 'The Importance of Elsewhere', the importance of difference, distance and strangeness, applies to poetic tradition as well as poetic imagination. Larkin had in a sense already visited Ireland by so thoroughly internalising Yeats. The story of modern poetry in these islands pivots on criss-crossings between Irish, British and American points of the aesthetic compass. Thus Larkin began

writing poetry at the intersection of several long-term and short-term
literary histories. These included the Irish Revival, modernism and
the poetry of the 1930s (W.H. Auden and Louis MacNeice). Further,
as regards Belfast literary culture, where these histories were also
about to be reactivated, Larkin arrived – and left – between the ebb-
ing of Hewitt's regionalism and the advent of new poets, in particular
Seamus Heaney, Derek Mahon and Michael Longley.

What links Larkin with these poets? The Belfast Group run by
Philip Hobsbaum in the early 1960s was certainly not the only
begetter of a new 'Northern Irish' poetry. But two conduits between
Larkin and the Group should be mentioned. First, Larkin's closest
literary friend in Belfast, the great polylingual, polymathic Arthur
Terry, who sadly died in February 2004, was a Group member: 'an
indispensable presence', to quote one obituarist. Second, Hobsbaum
took many of his own bearings from Larkin. But Hobsbaum read
Larkin in fairly simple social-realist terms. For more profound
assimilation we must look to Larkin's presence in the first collections
of the three poets named above. First, as I have said, Larkin's
example encouraged poets to be true to their own stirrings rather
than to fixed ideas about poetry's subject-matter or about where it
might be written. In that sense, regional and provincial horizons
merge and metropolises become irrelevant. Second, Larkin's
influence is most deeply embedded at a formal level, and the formal
level is where influence most deeply counts. All three poets are
noted for their reworking of traditional forms. And while other
precursors also mattered, Larkin was their most immediate model for
how traditional forms might negotiate the world of 1960. Following
on from MacNeice and Auden, he brought Yeats up to date. Perhaps
he realised his impact. Larkin chaired the committee which gave the
three poets I have named Eric Gregory awards (a UK award for poets
under thirty) in the mid-1960s. Writing to Arthur Terry he said that
he liked seeing 'those fresh young Irish faces'. Fresh, alas, no longer.

Of course, the world of 1960 was to change utterly in Belfast. And
when some critics later chided Northern Ireland's poets for not
tackling the 'Troubles' in more direct or *engagé* ways, Larkin's
aesthetic example, reductively termed 'the well-made poem', would
sometimes be blamed for depoliticising them in advance (Larkin as

perfide Albion's secret weapon). That is, most poets went on responding to what stirred their imaginations rather than to critical or political pundits 'telling chaps what to do'. They did not give up on poetic complexity, on 'the formal distancing of emotion'. One of Philip Larkin's legacies to Belfast literary culture, then, is that we have fewer bad Troubles poems than might otherwise be the case.

ABBREVIATIONS

CP Philip Larkin, *Collected Poems*, ed. Anthony Thwaite (London: Faber, 1988)

FR Philip Larkin, *Further Requirements: Interviews, Broadcasts, Statements and Book Reviews*, ed. Anthony Thwaite (London: Faber, 2001)

RW Philip Larkin, *Required Writing: Miscellaneous Pieces 1955–1982* (London: Faber, 1983)

SL *Selected Letters of Philip Larkin 1940–1985*, ed. Anthony Thwaite (London: Faber, 1992)

Six Poems

VÉNUS KHOURY-GHATA

Translated from the French by Theo Dorgan

I

A star
is a flame's invention
the whim of a spark
a lamp's opinion as it yearns for eternity
a clandestine manoeuvre of God's
revealed in the dictionaries.

The Yellow Nib, Vol. 1, 2005, pp 30–5

II

My mother would plunge herself deep in the breathless
movement of her broom,
battling the sand she called desert,
the damp she called crumbly water,
pond.

Her sweeping hands in remote places
would exhume the invisible dead
track the slightest weakening in a breeze
the least speck of obscurity,
sweeping with such self-sacrifice
bursting out laughing in gusts
for fear of appearing shrewish.

Mother so modest,
how little glory you drew from that wind
blowing only for your sweeping arms.

III

for May Ménassa

We were taught to distrust the voices that pierced the snow
on a set date
to address us from left to right
as if we came from the dark side of earth,
from the wrong side of the alphabet,

as if our walls would shelter the outdoors,
defend the interests of the cold,
protect the naked space of one dressed in saltpetre.

Unrecognisable, pressed against our windows, the faces
  of the seasons.
They claimed to be captive in our mirrors,
audience in our silent theatre.

We gave them our used clothes, we gave them
the leftovers from our savourless meals.

It was all empty flourish and make-believe,
the house an illusion,
its beams reflecting the streetlights,
and the chestnut tree endlessly repeating the same text
in the face of the wind, vain prompter.

An air of decay which well suited our mother's pallid linen,
the elevated palaver of father chatting to God through the
  open skylight.
Theatre of illusion, of feigned infatuation
where all that was real was the agony of the Crucified
climbing down off the wall at set times,
the mark of his torn arms indelible on the plaster.

IV

We have explained our despair to the thorn and the juniper,
Our only cousins in this foreign language;
We have cried on the pomegranate's shoulder,
Every month as it bleeds on our doorstep.

We have demanded audience of the forest,
Furnished the testimony of a pair of blackbirds
Whom we have seen scribble the word 'goat'
In both its senses,
We have vanquished the alphabet.

Our cobbler spoke Sanskrit,
The parish priest and the stream murmured in Latin;

They would reproach us for our ignorance of ornithology –
And yet we knew the name of every star, its exact
punctuation mark on the page of the sky.

V

Our cries, she used say,
Would score the glass panes of the moon
And scratch the angles of those tombs
Drawing milk down from the moon.

My mother would show us the long slope of her back
the better to interrogate damp marks on the wall,
decipher the crumbling alphabet of saltpetre,
translate the signs inscribed on the wrong side
of the town she knew only by its silhouette,
never venturing beyond the range of her shopping bag,
rarely overstepping
the timid limits of her lamp.

This town gave us nothing except its left-over rain
And sometimes a powdery snow, its flakes soft in the ears
of the pomegranate.

We have to clean the planet,
we have to wash God –
My mother's battlecry, buckling on her apron.

VI

I write 'Mother':
an old woman rises in the uncertain evening,
puts on a wedding dress,
climbs up onto the window sill
and calls out to the hostile city;
she addresses herself to the haughty streetlamps,
bares her breasts to the clocks,
showing them the precise location of her sorrow,
she undresses gently, for fear of creasing her wrinkles,
for fear of undermining the air.

There is a smell of frost in my mother's pockets,
And three stones for breaking the windows of summer;
My mother's dress has drunk all the snow of November,
The cries of dead birds have ripped out its hem.

TRANSLATOR'S NOTE

Vénus Khoury-Ghata was born in the Lebanese mountain village of Bsherre in 1937.
Her debut publication appeared in 1966, since when she has published poetry and
novels copiously. Awards include the Prix Supervielle for *Anthologie Personnelle*
(1997), an anthology of her poetry compiled by herself from which the poems
translated here are taken.

21 Clooneen for Maureen

MEDBH McGUCKIAN

Because you were never there I grew to know your house quite well. It was not better but it was something. I remembered fully where it was, what you had to look out at, if you ever looked out. The first time I went there the back gate was bolted. The second, it was not. The front post-box was not locked and then it was, with a twist of wire and a nail. The first time I thought of your hands constructing it, sawing the material, securing it. It was homespun, uneven, the edges rough. After spending hours and weeks trimming things to perfection, was it now your luxury to leave unsmoothed?

It is a back-to-front house, as some children's hearts are born. When you drive into the communal parking area, the back is what naturally presents itself, though the gate is there to the garden, whereas in a real house it is to the front. (By real I do not mean your house is not real, just that you were not there.) As I have thought of it a whole year now with you inhabiting it. The front has to be the front because it has an overhanging porch, where I stood for a few moments the second time, away from the spray of light summer rain, hoping that because I had to stay, had an excuse to stay, you might arrive like a ghost and be disturbed by my waiting. But not to give you too obvious a chance, I moved around the outside of the house while it continued raining, to show how little I cared.

It is not a place I could ever warm to or like. The other end of town is too grand, hedges and high walls and swept pavements. Gradually you go down, as always, past the police station, to the road-nipples and garages and corner Spars. Before today I had always felt in going down that I was going up. But today there was no further

The Yellow Nib, Vol. 1, 2005, pp 36–7

down I could go, alone, there was no sense of direction left in me.
The curl in the street and all those sharpnesses cut me equally. Boxes
and boxes, square after square, the stamp of grass without flowers a
choiceless green. Because I was the prisoner locked out who looked
at barred doors and tried to look through them. I counted the
windows like minutes and the bedroom one to the left was not ajar
and then it was. The curtains not meeting, you were not sleeping. I
learned the grain of each door by pressing lightly against its frame, so
frail I could not be broken by breaking. Cheap and woodless wood
that before I did not disdain because you were woodier. More wood.
Tree enough to make any door being swung back disappear, richer by
your voice turning its key.

How the drawn curtains drew me your hands again. How the
furniture posed where you did not need it. Each inch of wall that you
burst and landscaped into. That you filled a bright lake of sink and a
fair hill of stair. That you soared a pillar of fireplace and a vaulted
ceiling of kitchen. That a long tangerine hall lined with Van Dyck
you switched your television. That room upon marbled room
followed your few steps. That the porch I sheltered in overlooked
half of that county and did not hold it conquering. That I would
brush those muslin flaws climbing as if on your wallpaper out of
cultivated pots.

Now I examine your roof, where it folds among other roofs,
numbering still as I delay down one footway and back up the other.
It is how you might visit a gravestone, sure the person is not there,
hoping the rain might revive her, wondering what is her errand, once
the murmur. That there is no organ remaining in the soil or the fist-
shaped eye.

The next-door neighbour pins out towels, her small boy who can
hardly walk almost begins to speak. The one embraceable in all the
gardens. As children carry a space away from all who think they own
it into their memories for life, I have loved your house so nakedly, the
woman who sees you lock yourself out and in, after I am gone, will
imagine the nude no longer over your bed is hers, is her.

Seven Poems

DAVID WHEATLEY

Mocker

The beach's naked
        then clothed again
                maja,
white-into-brown,
        brown-into-white
                again mocha:
the waves' kiss
        forever short
                of the machair.

The Owl

after Baudelaire

Owl at my window, window owl,
under the sycamore's midnight eaves,
alien god whose red eye roves
while he sits tight and plays it cool.

No police copter or car alarm
can budge him from his airy perch,
unflappable, who must keep watch
until the hour of perfect calm.

Look and learn: don't just do
something, stand there. Stand still and be wise.
Be the owl who does as he pleases.

Drunk on every passing shadow
man will always pay the price
for having wanted to change places.

A Stone Head

'The wretched man 'gan grinning horridlie' – Spenser

Here's one for Dr Spurzheim's
phrenological cabinet,
Palaeolithic department:

the coroner's chisel records
no purchase on this stone
head's flinty bump

of amativeness, waked
from its bottom-drawer guillotine
basket by the attendant

and placed before us, bowling
ball, cannonball good
for any target in sight,

the thin nose tracing a plumbline
behind the eyes, frank
as the handwritten dates where the neck

gives way, curling from sealed
lips a broad, devouring,
laughably absent grin.

Dear Incomprehension,
It's Thanks to You...

... I've understood so much, have made a fool of myself so wisely and so well. You may turn over and go back to sleep, I announce to the Sports Hall, returning to sleep, me too, to uneventful dreams, at best. For 'Sign here in blood' read 'Scrawl a happy face in leaking red biro', for 'Your life and mine depend on this' read 'How much longer till opening time?' Marks will be deducted for scoring marks. When you go to the bathroom I note it all down, commit it to memory: bowel movements costive, costive, then sudden, then sluice-like, out it all comes, cascading, just like the answers to all this rubbish. Look at the mess I've made of this page, dripping in – what is this stuff? I've no idea. Now wash your hands. Once I too had questions to answer, would sit here sucking my pencil and sweating; now I sit for hours writing nothing and know this is progress, and they know it too, my gum-chewing charges. While waiting I hunch down and try my hand at marbles along the aisles, my prize bottler scattering all in its path. I giggle at the squeak of my shoes on the floor and hide under a desk, seeing you coming. So come and get me, if that's what you want, I can't be so hard to find with a backside like mine, sticking out, not to mention the smell. What a good job the Brothers did on me, I've an answer for everything. Ventriloquist, I can throw my voice too: that spotty boy in the corner, he's telling you to form an orderly queue for conversion of scripts into paper aeroplanes, and he means it too. Whoosh! there goes one now. Then in no time I'm alone again with all these empty desks and an abandoned good-luck muppet sprawled over a chair. Student number, exam number? No response. Question one? No response. Someone hasn't been paying attention. I rap my fingers, louder, louder, at this rate we'll be here all night, and I don't care much for your attitude either. Then I trip on a marble, go tumbling into your lap, whose lap, no one's, the spotty boy has washed his hands of me, I was the dummy all along, I lie mouthing impotent words on the floor, feeling around for my tongue. They'll never let me resit this one, not now, not ever; they stamp my paper *summa cum laude*, one hundred per cent, and throw me out in disgrace, and the truth is I've understood nothing, nothing, my pockets still full of marbles and a paper plane in my ear, I always did so well in exams, as a boy.

A Great Strapping Lad With Terrible Teeth
for my father

The toothpaste tube is broken-backed almost beyond use, hatching worms of its pinky dough in all directions while I contort one last pellet onto my brush. We never discuss toothpaste, you and I, the finer points of this pungent goo, but it is toothpaste the factory makes on Pottery Road, toothpaste it was making those nights I pulled up outside the gates to drive you home. And here it is now on my bathroom sink and foaming in my mouthful of yellow malformities.

Sitting in Dr Flood's chair as a child, I watched the bluetits flock to his window and thought of the mercury puzzle out in his waiting room, the teardrops of my concentration dripping along its mazy corridors. I sat in the chair and watched the birds and bit on my dental impression. The only known predator on the beast in my mouth is this brace, getting its teeth into mine, slowly, slowly, over the years, in vain. I bare my fangs at myself in simultaneous menace and fear.

Travelling, leaving home, I pack my toothpaste and on arrival find it has leaked, trailing its slime all over my washbag. The flotsam of my dinner collects in my crossed front teeth, coming off on my finger and going back in my mouth. That's what I call appetite. And so it is that in the name of cleanliness I only succeed in making things worse.

Still there's a tube of your toothpaste to be had at the Co-op, even here. Today when you call you will have been out since break of day until now, the night now falling, working. In your hand you will have a glass and faintly I will hear the fur of red wine on your teeth, the fur on your voice, and be glad.

I snip the tube in two and squeeze out the dregs of the paste. When I draw up at the factory next my parking will be woeful as ever, count on that much. But we never discuss toothpaste, you and I, it just never comes up. There's nothing more to be had from the tube. Out with it, into the bin. Pink in the bathroom mirror my scoured and sorry tongue shows its cheeky flag of shame.

Or, The Road Movie

YOU ARE NOW ENTERING

twinned
with

welcomes careful drivers

| 10,000 Lakes | First in Flight | Stars Fell On |

I wish my girlfriend was as dirty as this

←

500 yards

E
  N
    D
      S

Taxation without Representation

H
O
U
R
L
Y

R
A
T
E
S

Wrong Way
Turn Around

Famous Potatoes

YOU ARE NOW LEAV

Come   back   soon!

Nationwide

The slow fuse　　　　amber and black
　　　　of match day's　　　three o'clock shout
　　　　　　　files past us
　　　along the bridge

everything　　in its right place
for an early season　　grudge tie
　　　Northern realism
　　　　　　v. estrangement effect

　　　　the cinder path　　　and the chimney
are certain starters　　the railway
has been deemed
　　　ineligible

there are crab apples　　　　　　in the garden
　　　　behind the hospital　and a domino
　　　　　　row of tower blocks
　　　　　　if required

the first side to give up　　　the struggle
　　　　will be declared　　victors
the crowd will be
　　　ferocious yet fair

　　　　its cheering follows us　　　up the street
as we make our way　　　home: a small
puppy dog　　we pick up
　　　and carry

　　　hours later　　taking the bin out
we find it　　running in circles
　　　in the back garden
　　　　　and think

           of the crab apple   harvest
perfect red inedible   going
        to waste and
              rightly so

Eleven Polish Poems

Translated from the Polish by Cathal McCabe

KONSTANTY ILDEFONS GAŁCZYŃSKI
1905–1953

From the River Limpopo:
A Letter

I write to you all from the River Limpopo
(the countries it runs through none of you'll know).
Outside my tent elephants walk
and red- and emerald-coloured folk.
I can see the crooked oil lamp that sways
above the table each night like a face
in a dream; the fat spiders sitting
in corners, knitting.
Each day you wait for the post. But who knocks?
Only the wireless, a polished box,
brings you 'concerts' – organ-blasts –
when an organ-army bursts
into the room, brandishing spears and threats.
It is then your old hearts
creak with fear,
like the door.
Each night a voice from the box declaims:
Tomorrow it is going to rain.
Here, though, huge stars – and huger rubies!
Little dark boys

The Yellow Nib, Vol. 1, 2005, pp 48–67

run up and pin back
the royal palanquin
and the King
of the River Limpopo himself calls for an uncut pack ...
while you sit with your poverty, boredom,
mice and rain back home.

1934

MIRON BIAŁOSZEWSKI
1922–1983

'And Even If, Even If,
They Take My Stove Away':
My Inexhaustible Ode to Joy

I have a stove
A triumphal arch of a stove!

They've come for my stove
My triumphal arch of a stove!!

Hands off my stove!
My triumphal arch of a stove!!!

But would they listen?

Now all I have is an
    empty
        gloomy
            gap
    empty gloomy gap

Which is more than enough:
empty gloomy gap
empty gloomy gap
emp-ty-gloo-my-gap
emptygloomygap!

WISŁAWA SZYMBORSKA
1923–

A Glass of Wine

His look said: *you're beautiful* –
and I took him at his word.
Happy, I swallowed a star.

I consented to being created
in the likeness of my reflection
in his eyes. I dance, dance
in a shuddering of sudden wings.

The table is a table, the wine wine
in a glass that is a glass
that, standing, stands on the table.
And I am an illusion,
an improbable illusion,
an illusion to the bone.

I say whatever he wants:
tell him of ants
that die of love,
the constellation
of a dandelion
above.
I swear that a white rose,
sprinkled with wine, will sing.

I laugh and tilt my head
to one side, as if I were testing
an invention. I dance, dance
in my astonished skin, in the arms of he
who created me.

Eve from a rib, Venus from foam,
Minerva from the head of Jove
were more real.

When he isn't looking in my direction
I search for my reflection
on the wall. And all I see,
where a picture was, is the nail.

TADEUSZ RÓŻEWICZ
1921–

Rain in Cracow

rain in Cracow
rain
falls on the Wawel Dragon
on the bones of giants
on Kościuszko's mound
on the statue of Mickiewicz
on Podkowiński's *Frenzy*
on Mr Dulski
on the bugle-call from the top of St Mary's

rain
rain in Cracow
falls on Skałka's whitening stone
on Błonie's green fields
on the Marshal's coffin
beneath silver bells
on his men in grey

clouds come down
settle on Cracow
rain
rain falls
on the eyes of Wyspiański
on his blind stained glass

a mild eye of sky
a bolt of blue

long-legged girls in wedge-heeled shoes
fold away brightly coloured umbrellas

it brightens up
out
comes the sun
I visit the monasteries
looking for the dance of death

in my room at the hotel
I try to stop
a poem about to fly away

I have pinned a butterfly
to the page
a gossamer-wing
a little blue stain

rain rain rain
in Cracow

I read Norwid
how sweet it is to fall asleep
sweeter still to be of stone

goodnight my dears
goodnight
poets alive and dead
poetry, goodnight

July 2000

ZBIGNIEW HERBERT
1924–1998

My City

The ocean arranges
a star of salt
on its bed

the air distils
shining stones

defective memory
plots a map of the city

a starfish of streets
the planets of far-off squares
gardens' green nebulae

in broken pointed helmets
emigrés lament matter's demise

from riddled chests
fall precious stones

I dreamt I was walking
from my parents' house to school
how could I not know the way?
to the left Pashanda's shop
another school bookshops
even old Bodek's head
there behind a window

I want to turn for the cathedral
when suddenly a shutter falls
the street is no more
I simply can go no further
yet I know for a fact
that this was never a cul-de-sac

the ocean of volatile memory
washes crushes images

in the end will remain
the stone on which I was born

each night
I stand barefoot
before the slammed gates
of my city

EDWARD STACHURA
1937–1979

Letter to Those Left Behind

I am dying
for my sins – and for my innocence
for the lack I feel in each cell of my body, each cell of my soul
for a lack that has me torn to shreds, like a newspaper covered
    with loud empty words
for the possibility of communion with the Unnamable,
    Inexpressible, Unknown
for the new day
for the wonders of itinerancy
for a view to beat all views
for a proper vision
for a dotted i
for the secret of death
        in danger, fear and the sweat of a brow
for mislaid certainties
for the lost keys of understanding
        with a tiny spark of trust that says, even if the seed
        dies, a fruit will come forth
for the loneliness of dying
for every body is a corpse
for it's trying, terrible, unendurable
for the possibility of a metamorphosis
for the unhappiness of others and my own which I carry inside
    and out
for it looks to have all been nothing but a dream, a nightmare
for it looks to have all been a lie
for it looks to have all been a farce
for everything here is decaying, rotting and all you have is a
    longing for something that lasts

for I am no longer of this world and maybe never was
for it seems there is no hope for me here
for earthly love is beyond me now
for *noli me tangere*
for I am very tired, weak beyond words
for I have been through a lot
for I have, although in madness, been literally, physically
    crucified and how truly and surely it hurt
for I wished to redeem the world and all in it from every evil,
    and if I failed, then it was no fault of mine
for it looks as though I'll leave nothing behind
for I do not feel cheated – that would allow me to go on rather
    than die; to go on and find the offender, myself maybe;
    but I do not feel cheated
for whosoever can live in this world – let him go on and I wish
    him good health, and when his turn to die comes round –
    let his death be light
for as for me, I am coming, Lord, to you, my shepherd
      perhaps at last to know peace
      deserved I have little doubt, deserved I have little doubt
for even insanity I was not spared
for the pain is fierce
[*illegible*]
for I am suffocating in this cage
for my soul is lonely so long as I live
for I have run out of paper right on time and it's only a step
    away and Long Live Life
for I stood at the beginning, for the Lord took my hand and I
    stand at the finish and taste not death.

RAFAŁ WOJACZEK
1945–1971

Death Has Yet to Find its Proper Expression

Though already the first snow is falling
My hair is growing yet

BOHDAN ZADURA
1945–

from Coffins from IKEA

I learnt to skate
aged twenty-eight,
was thirty before I could swim
and then for a long time
nothing …
                    till a month ago: IKEA

Before you will open
a dark forest of light pine,
Ariadne's help-
ing hand your only hope …
Your eyes go in all directions at once
(like your legs on the ice rink once)
and your head spins
at the sight of so many curtains
and cushions, pillows and covers,
the stripes and checks, duvets and cupboards
wardrobes closets every size of box
tumblers basins teapots clocks
bells chimes tables stools
handles screws hinges tools
lamps candles frames tassels cords
armchairs benches and skirting- and skirting- and skirting-boards
reeling, a forest, before your eyes
as in Soviet films when the hero, struck by a fascist bullet, dies
and/or swoons in the arms of the nurse
And then – of course! –
it clicked:
the one thing they lacked

and I thought that if she
were the one to bury me
and they were here on sale
at least in that misfortune she'd find some pleasure still

ZDZISŁAW JASKUŁA
1951–

Soft as the Light

Huddled in fear
on the bank of night
I found you

in the light of my gaze
you arose

you walked with me then
arms apart
tender
at peace
soft as the light
we enter

now we walk through the most exquisite dawn

of our love
not a word

Summer 1968

JERZY JARNIEWICZ
1958–

Poem

you can burn your fingers
in the black flame that lingers

after you've put
the candle out

MARCIN SENDECKI
1967–

Carpathian Days

I might have known: *You want to go on Monday?*
Me, I'd go on another day. The usual superstition. Or lack of organisation.
I could have gone on another day, but Monday I'm at the stadium,
watching the wonderful world go by. A man with no legs
by a booth, a woman beneath an umbrella. (This the view from the stall.)
Then, all of a sudden, here comes the bus.

There's nothing worse than a broken-down bus.
If it doesn't conk out, we'll be there after dark, on Tuesday.
So fingers crossed that the engine not stall.
National Express: the last word in organisation!
On the train at least you can stretch your legs.
Nobody knows if we stop in Garwolin.

We didn't. But we've fifteen minutes in Ryki.
My neighbour gets out for a fag, then walks around the bus.
Across the aisle a girl sips a Coke, legs
in the air, ugly as sin. She's not going back till Wednesday
when her man goes into the army. Which calls for the organisation
of vodka, some chairs and a stool.

A driver needs to have nerves of steel.
One false move and instead of the station in Lublin
we stop for good at the mortuary. *What kind of an organisation*
– this, next day, in the papers – *lets an hysteric drive its bus?*
We'll be an item till Thursday,
at least. On the evening news my corpse, its legs.

Alive, we drive on. The girl sits so I can see her legs
then covers them – damn! – along with the scars where the little steel
pins (or needles) went in. Her neighbour suggests they go out some
     night, Friday
he picks up his wage. They could spend the weekend in Krasnystaw,
two whole days! Immediately everyone sat on the bus
gives a cheer. We're all one happy family, one well-oiled organisation.

It's getting late. – *The driver is taking some corners!* – *Every organisation*
chokes in the end on itself, kicks the proverbial bucket. Both legs.
Same with memory. Just you wait. Years on, the bus
sways beneath a great magnet, today shards of memory, shards of steel.
Till when I'm sat at the station in Zamosc.
Till then! (Then being this coming Saturday.)

If I show up. To think of the organisation involved in exchanging
     addresses!
Some Monday, no doubt, I'll throw this piece of paper away. Legless,
     no doubt, in Tomaszów.
Leant against the bus, with a damp cigarette, I'll watch the wind seize
     it – and lose it in style.

Miron Białoszewski (1922–1983) was born in Warsaw. A poet, prose writer and dramatist, he studied Polish at the underground University of Warsaw and lived through the Warsaw Uprising, an experience he describes in his book, *Pamiętnik z Powstania Warszawskiego* (published in English as *A Memoir of the Warsaw Uprising*). After the war he worked as a journalist and in 1955 set up his own theatre with friends, writing and performing plays in a flat in Warsaw. The poem translated here, ' "Ach, gdyby, gdyby nawet piec zabrali..." Moja niewyczerpana oda do radości', is from the poet's first collection, *Obroty rzeczy* (1956).

Konstanty Ildefons Gałczyński (1905–1953) was born in Warsaw. Having spent the early 1930s in Berlin and Vilnius and the war as a prisoner in the German camps of Mühlberg and Altengrabow, he returned to live in Poland until his death in 1953. *Collected Works*, comprising poetry, prose writings, dramatic works and translations, appeared in 1979. *Selected Works* was published in 2002 to mark the fiftieth anniversary of the poet's death. The poem translated here, 'List znad rzeki Limpopo', was first collected in *Utwory poetyckie* (1937).

Zbigniew Herbert (1924–1998) is one of the most translated Polish poets. He was born and grew up in Lvov, where he studied Polish at the underground Jan Kazimierz University. He settled in Paris in 1986 but returned to Warsaw in 1992, where he remained until his death in 1998. 'My City' (original title 'Moje miasto') is taken from the poet's second collection, *Hermes, pies i gwiazda* [Hermes, Dog and Star] (1957).

Jerzy Jarniewicz (1958–   ) was born in Łowicz. The author of six volumes of poetry, his *Selected Poems* appeared in 2000. A lecturer at the universities of Łódź and Warsaw, and an editor with *Literatura na Świecie* [World Literature], he is one of Poland's leading critics and translators of English-language poetry and fiction. He is currently working on a new Polish translation of *A Portrait of the Artist as a Young Man*. He lives in Łódź. 'Poem' (original title 'Wiersz') was first published in *Sa rzeczy których nie ma* (1995).

Zdzisław Jaskuła (1951–   ) was born in Łask and studied Polish at the universities of Łódź and Lublin. He has worked as a director with various theatres including Teatr Nowy in Łódź. Among his volumes of poetry are early underground collections and *Maszyna do pisania* (1984), from which 'Soft as the Light' ('Łagodne jak światło') is taken. He lives in Łódź.

Tadeusz Różewicz (1921–   ) was born and grew up in Radomsko. His first collection of poetry, *Niepokój* (1947), registered the guilt and incredulity of a survivor of the war and heralded the arrival of a major and original poetic voice. After the war he studied History of Art at the Jagiellonian University before settling in Silesia in 1949. Apart from many volumes of poetry, he has also published a large body of dramatic work and several collections of prose writings. Previously untranslated, 'Rain in Cracow' ('Deszcz w Krakowie') concludes the 2001 volume *nożyk profesora* [The Professor's Knife].

Marcin Sendecki (1967–   ) was born in Gdańsk and studied Sociology at the University of Warsaw. Formerly on the editorial board of the quarterly *bruLion*, he has published six collections of poetry and co-edited (with fellow poets Marcin Baran and Marcin Świetlicki) an anthology of poems, *Długie pożegnanie: Tribute to Raymond Chandler*. He lives in Warsaw. 'Carpathian Days' ('Dni kultury karpackiej') appeared in *Szkoci Dół* (2002).

Edward Stachura (1937–1979) was born to Polish parents in Pont-de-Chéry, France, and came to Poland aged eleven. A poet, prose writer, singer-songwriter and translator, he travelled for much of his life throughout Poland, Europe, America, Mexico and the Middle East. Written shortly before he committed suicide, 'Letter to Those Left Behind' ('List do

Pozostałych') concludes his posthumously published five volume *Collected Works* (1982), comprising poems, songs, translations, stories, novels and diaries.

Wisława Szymborska (1923–   ) was born in Bnin, near Poznań. She studied Polish and Sociology at the Jagiellonian University, and her entire life has been closely connected with Cracow, where she still lives. She worked for many years as an editor of the literary magazine *Życie literackie*. In 1996 she was awarded the Nobel Prize for Literature. 'A Glass of Wine' (original title 'Przy winie') is taken from her second collection, *Sól* [Salt] (1962).

Rafał Wojaczek (1945–1971) was born in the Silesian town of Mikołów. He briefly studied Polish at the Jagiellonian University before settling in Wrocław, where he committed suicide at the age of twenty-five. His *Collected Works* appeared posthumously in 1976. Something of a cult figure in the years following his death, he is represented in many anthologies, including the two-volume *Od Staffa do Wojaczka: Poezja polska 1939–1985* (1988). Lech Majewski's biographical film, *Wojaczek*, was released in 1999. A new *Collected Poems* is published in 2005 by Biuro Literackie, Wrocław. The poem translated here, 'Śmierc nie znalazła jeszcze właściwego wyrazu', was first collected in *Ktorego nie bylo* (1972 [posthumous]).

Bohdan Zadura (1945–   ) was born in Puławy, where he continues to live and work as a poet, prose-writer, literary critic and translator of English, American, Irish, Hungarian, Ukrainian and Russian poetry. A graduate of the University of Warsaw, he has worked in the Kazimierz Dolny Regional Museum and for the literary periodicals *Tworczość*, *Akcent* and *Literatura na Świecie* [World Literature]. His many volumes of poetry include the acclaimed *Cisza* [Silence] (1994) and *Ptasia grypa* [Bird Flu] (2002), from which 'Coffins from IKEA' ('Trumny z Ikei') is taken. The first volume of his *Collected Poems* has recently been published by Biuro Literackie, Wrocław.

The Winter's Tale

MAUREEN BOYLE

1
Emilia

I could not stanch her body that first night
when it seemed that every part of it was weeping.
She was sluiced all right and by no near neighbour.

I could not find her eyes – so lost were they in the flow of face
that seemed to melt as I looked into it
swollen in grief, animate, fluent with tears.

Her breasts wept too – azure veined and beautiful –
we padded them with cabbage leaves as the older women said
and bathed her in a bath of borrowed water.

This was no queen's chamber of her own
where white linen and flowers were readied for her welcome,
her withdrawal, her privacy, away from men.

This place was dark, piss-stinking – a heifer stall
where her calf came early and lusty,
'from one prison to another,' her mother said.

She would feed this child herself
as if knowing this was all she could impart before the severance.
It drank her in – the queen turned wet-nurse.

The Yellow Nib, Vol. 1, 2005, pp 68–76
© Maureen Boyle

Where her daughter came she bled and we saved the child's
    packing
to bury under a winter thorn where Paulina said,
something of this little one would blossom from the dead.

When the child was gone she seemed to leave us too
    delirious and dreaming,
she was going out to give the child a name and when we leaned in
    close to hear,
it was the name of the lost, 'Perdita', that came.

2
Hermione
The Winding Sheet

I dream I am lying dead in a yellow monastery
that sits on a hill against a sky blue as imperial sapphire.
The emperor of Russia was my father and this may be Ipatiev
he told me of – I can see the place where I am dead.

They are laying me out – the women
working in silence to the sound of vespers rising from below.
In a stripped bare cell that is beautiful,
I can see this place where I am dead.

The cell is washed in the weak light of winter dusk
in the yellow monastery where the early sunset
blazes on the dome. My father was emperor of Russia
and I feel I have come home.

I am royal infant once again – naked and in care
of women's hands – my body never loved like this in life,
they work in rhythm with the chant – along my legs,
   along my arms
tenderly they tend me – I am not alarmed.

I am not afraid of death where I lie
in the silence of the yellow monastery,
these women love me, and my winding sheet
smells of blue winter air and of rosemary.

The vigil of the night gives way to dawn
with matins comes the sound of Russian bells.
Underneath the Mother-of-God icon
I can see the place where I am dead.

I am lying dead in the yellow monastery
on top of the blue-crowned hill.
The emperor of Russia was my father,
in Ipatiev I lie cold and still.

3
Waking

I

I wake into the hardest winter I have known
withdrawn into myself as to a cloister.
I watch the world from the widow's walk of Paulina's home
high above the town.

In this frozen time, in blue columns on windless days
smoke from the small houses rises straight to heaven,
and I fly back down those chimneys to the hearths,
envying the women who can smell their children's heads.

I cannot remember how my children smelled.

On damp days the smoky stench of cinders rises
from the same fires and all is drenched and dripping
like the trees, and I spend hours gazing and trying not to think –
my heart tuned to the tick of the clock in the darkened room,
my soul slowed to the thick time I must live through.

II

Sometimes I go out in disguise,
descend the hill from Paulina's house
and take the river way where everything is frozen.
Geese cross the winter sky and a lonely heron
keeps me company on the river.

She is marked in splendid greys,
her plumage always a surprise
against the drabness of the day.
Ahead of me, the birds that haunt the temples of the dead,
goldfinches, lace my way, flash like firelight in the gloom.

III

Where is my child?

I feel she has been taken from the earth,
banished in the blackness of her father's words –
too dark for a little child to bear.
She is like one of those ill-born, misshapen,
a moon-child that slips away too soon
and is buried at the edge of things,

unmarked.

4
The Anchoress

It is fitting that he thinks that I have died
and we decide to leave things like this
for in a way I have. Paulina will watch and manage
his slow, sweet penance and I will stay hidden,
like the woman of the Rhine I read about.

At Disibodenberg she wore a shroud,
lay prostrate on the chapel floor
and entered the blessed cell
to the sound of her own funeral antiphon
and the canticles of the dead.

But in that tomb she sees things with an inner eye –
visions of cities and heaven in the sky.
We will make of my life such a revolving door,
a *fenestra versatilis* where sustenance and sacraments
can pass but I will stay unseen, immured.

5
The Quickening

At first I kept a winter garden, which mocked me –
it was full of things changing form and dying:
the seeds of nasturtiums paled,
darkened and hardened into little skulls;
the heads of poppies were rattling noisy censers;
the ground a tracery of better seasons.

But then something in the year quickened.
After the equinox the healing witch-plant spidered into bloom
and bulbs crowning in the ground pushed
blushing crimson tips into a wintry gloom.
The 'prickbush' had its first leaves, purple and soft as
    a baby's fontanelle.
The hellebore, pale as a morning moon, drifted into flower.

As the soil warmed I could begin to finger it
and find the palimpsest of other gardens.
I found the eggs of things blanched by the dark
like the seeds of the apple of Carthage drained of their blood,
and I wondered what seeds my baby would eat underground,
that would seal her sentence and keep her away from me.

Venus is the goddess of small gardens but I am Ceres here,
whose daughter has been swallowed up,
where the earth opened under a blue narcissus.

This garden is my meditation,
and shadows tell the office of the day.
A robin comes and stands at my feet,
a blackbird is silhouetted against the sky,
his song in the pine tree choiring the hours,
mixing with the voices of Paulina's girls at play.

6
Recovery

I am my own richness.

This ruched silk rustles.
It is the colour of pomegranate flesh
or of the broad-bean flowers.
I glow and smoulder in it.

The sun burns upon this page.
I close my eyes under my hat
and let the noises of the day
drift over me:

pine cones falling into water;
the intimate buzzing of a bee;
the rhythmic beating of rugs from a balcony;
and everywhere – cicadas.

There is nothing more lovely
than the vista of a morning,
long and languid, and I am woman,
storing up this day
against the coming bleakness
of the winter.

The End of the Poem

Final lecture as holder of the Oxford Chair of Poetry
4 May 2004

PAUL MULDOON

'Welsh Incident' by Robert Graves
'A Failure' by C. Day-Lewis
'Keeping Going' by Seamus Heaney

> Since my election to the venerable Oxford Chair of Poetry, I have often been mistaken for a respectable public figure, and four American universities have recently wanted to make me their guest poet. I declined politely.

So Robert Graves begins his provocative 1963 lecture, 'Nine Hundred Iron Chariots'. And so he continues:

> Though my Oxford obligations are no great burden, and can be annually settled in two months or less, I grudge every hour spent away from my home among the rocks and olives of Majorca, except on important business. Yet among my latest preoccupations has been a wish to discover the mystique behind modern science: so, on being invited to spend two weeks on the MIT campus as the Arthur D. Little Lecturer, I thought: 'This is it! Nowhere in the world can a more massive concentration of scientific thought be found than at MIT. Let me pretend for once that I am a respectable public figure, and investigate.'

In my final lecture in this series, I'd like to investigate three poems by three Irish poets, all respectable public figures who held the Chair of Poetry at Oxford and who, in these three poems at least, are

The Yellow Nib, Vol. 1, 2005, pp 77–99

concerned with 'mystique' and 'science', with difficulty and the coming to terms with difficulty, with problems and their solutions. The poem itself is, after all, the solution to a problem only it has raised, and our reading of it necessarily entails determining what that problem was. Only then may we determine the extent to which it has, or has not, succeeded. That is the only decent end of the poem, and our only decent end is to let the poem have its way with us, just as the poet let it have its way with him or her. Robert Graves goes on to the give a blow-by-blow account of this shamanistic experience:

> Symptoms of the trance in which poetic composition occurs differ greatly from those of an induced mediumistic trance; though both seem directed by an external power. In a poetic trance, which happens no more predictably than a migraine or an epileptic fit, this power is traditionally identified with the ancient Muse-goddess. All poems, it seems, grow from a small verbal nucleus gradually assuming an individual rhythm and verse form. The writing is not 'automatic', as in a mediumistic trance when the pen travels without pause over the paper, but is broken by frequent critical amendments and excisions. And though the result of subsequently reading a poem through may be surprise at the unifying of elements drawn from so many different levels of consciousness, this surprise will be qualified by dissatisfaction with some lines. Objective recognition of the poem as an entity as a rule then induces a lighter trance, during which the poet realizes more fully the implications of his lines, and sharpens them. The final version (granted the truthfulness of its original draft, and the integrity of any secondary elaboration) will hypnotize readers who are faced by similar problems into sharing the poet's emotional experience.

The key to Graves's notion of 'trance' is that both writer and reader are involved in it. Both are 'hypnotized'. Writer and reader blend into one indivisible function. Where their ends meet is itself indivisible from – might even be thought of as the definition of – the end of the poem. It's not a new idea, of course – one thinks of Ralph Waldo Emerson's assertion that 'there is creative reading as well as creative writing' – but it's an idea that has not so far had the currency it might. Both writer-as-reader and reader-as-writer meet at the interface between what is recognisable and what is new, negotiating as they do the to-and-fro between familiar and strange, both operating somewhere between the primary ecstatic state and the 'secondary elaboration', as Graves describes it. That negotiation might be said to be at the heart of the 'Welsh Incident', and is fore-grounded as early as the first word of the title. As Graves surely knew, the word 'Welsh' derives from the Anglo-Saxon *wylisc*, 'a foreigner', and is particularly appropriate to a poem whose subject matter is 'all sorts of queer things'.

We need to spend a little time with the title, if only because it's not the title under which the poem was first published in *Poems, 1929*, where it appeared as 'Railway Carriage'. The title as we have it, then, was written not *through* Graves the primary ecstatic but *by* Graves the secondary elaborator. One may begin to understand why the secondary elaborator thought he was on the right track, as it were, in changing the title when we consider that the other major change Graves made to the poem when it appeared in *Collected Poems, 1938* was in the description of the noise made by the 'the most odd, indescribable thing of all' and the 'something recognizably a something' that it did. In the first version of the poem, the something it did was to emit 'a loud belch'. Douglas Day notes in *Swifter than Reason*, his study of the poetry and criticism of Graves, how the poet, 'moved by an inexplicable and uncharacteristic niceness, changed the belch to "a very loud, respectable noise – like groaning to oneself on Sunday morning in Chapel" – thereby robbing the poem of a large degree of its humour'.

What was going on in Graves's mind when he made these revisions? The answer is at once 'too much' and 'not enough'. In dropping the title 'Railway Carriage' we all but entirely lose the context of the dialogue of which the poem is made up, the setting of this rambling conversation. 'Railway Carriage' may not be the most scintillating title in the history of poetry in English, but it's certainly no less scintillating than the new title, which threatens redundancy. There's surely no doubt that the setting of the poem is in Wales and that it describes, in its own way, an 'incident', that's to say 'something that occurs casually in the course of, or in connection with, something else, of which it constitutes no essential part' (OED). The word 'incident' sends us back, not unrewardingly, to our great

poet of 'incidents' (including 'Incident at Bruges' [my emphasis]).
William Wordsworth's sonorous blank verse will be confirmed as
being a model here by the time we get to the end of the first line or
two of 'Welsh Incident':

> But that was nothing to what things came out
> From the sea-caves of Criccieth yonder.

This sends me back, not only in its prosody but in its 'sea-beast'
imagery, to the first description of the leech-gatherer in
Wordsworth's 'Resolution and Independence':

> As a huge stone is sometimes seen to lie
> Couched on the bald top of an eminence;
> Wonder to all who do the same espy,
> By what means it could thither come, and whence;
> So that it seems a thing endued with sense:
> Like a sea-beast crawled forth, that on a shelf
> Of rock or sand reposeth, there to sun itself.

These Wordsworthian 'things' ('the things which I have seen I now
can see no more') are distinctly un-Wordsworthian in that they offer
no 'Intimations of Immortality' nor any kind of 'help', as with the
sturdy 'leech-gatherer on the lonely moor' and the steadfast, all but
static, 'Old Cumberland Beggar' – 'Him even the slow-paced waggon
leaves behind'.

That image of the 'slow-paced waggon' reminds me of another
major source in 'Railway Carriage', if we may continue to call it that
for a moment, since I still haven't left my discussion of the title. I'm
thinking, of course, of the unreliable correspondent in Robert Frost's
'The Mountain' (1914), who, not unlike the old Cumberland beggar,
was 'a man who moved so slow / With white-faced oxen, in a heavy
cart, / It seemed no harm to stop him altogether'. Like 'Railway
Carriage', 'The Mountain' is a dramatic poem, in which the poem's
protagonist and the teamster-testifier keep glancing off each other
ineffectually before what might be described as the poetic equivalent
of a slow fade to black:

'You've lived here all your life?'

                         'Ever since Hor

Was no bigger than a —————' What, I did not hear.

He drew the oxen toward him with light touches

Of his slim goad on nose and offside flank,

Gave them their marching orders and was moving.

We see immediately how Frost's poem rolls to a halt in precisely the same way as Graves's, with its 'I was coming to that'. What's intriguing about the relationship between Graves and Frost is the extent to which their influence was mutual. When Frost first came to England, one of the poets by whom he was most inspired was Graves, whom he would meet in the autumn of 1914, the very year in which 'The Mountain' was collected in *North of Boston*. Graves would go on to edit a selection of Frost's poems, and to describe him as 'the first American who could be honestly reckoned a master-poet by world standards'. When he met Frost, Graves had just been commissioned as an officer in the Royal Welch Fusiliers, so that component of the '*Welsh* Incident' [my emphasis] has a resonance above and beyond his childhood associations with Harlech. So closely are *Fairies and Fusiliers* connected in Graves's mind that it is the title of a book of poems published in 1917, in which we read 'Letter to S.S.':

You'll see where in old Roman Days,

Before revivals changed our ways,

The Virgin 'scaped the Devil's grab,

Printing her foot on a stone slab

With five clear toe-marks; and you'll find

The fiendish thumbprint close behind.

You'll see where Math, Mathonwy's son,

Spoke with the wizard Gwydion

And had him for South Wales set out

To steal that creature with the snout,

That new-discovered grunting beast

Divinely flavoured for the feast.

No traveler yet has hit upon

A wilder land than Meirion,

For desolate hills and tumbling stones,
Bogland and melody and old bones.
Fairies and ghosts are here galore,
And poetry most splendid, more
Than can be written with the pen
Or understood by common men.

In an interview with Leslie Norris published in the *Listener* of 28 May
1970, Graves explained his interest in this land of 'ghosts and fairies':

> My father was an Irish bard who was attached to the Eisteddfod; and
> he was one of the group who helped to start the Welsh Folk-Song
> Society. I used to go with my sister through the hill country behind
> Harlech; we had one of those wax phonographs and used it to
> collect Welsh folk-songs. Unfortunately, those were the days before
> cassettes and other instruments. All we had was the phonograph,
> and my sister, who was a musician, would note down what we had
> recorded – and then we had to rewax the cylinder. We had only
> one. It was a great pity because we lost the actual singing voice, and
> that's important. You get all the gracenotes.

Something of the tenderness with which Graves recounts this
ethnomusicologist childhood is evident in his account of the aurality
of the experiences at the heart of the 'very loud respectable noise' of
'Welsh Incident' or 'a loud belch' in 'Railway Carriage'. It is related
partly to 'the grunting beast' in 'Letter to S.S.'. The 'aurality', or lack
of it, is reminiscent of the end of 'The Mountain'. There, the last bit
of information given by Frost's teamster-testifier is not actually heard
by the protagonist, but might as well be a 'belch' like the one
expurgated from 'Welsh Incident'. The fact that the 'belch' has
disappeared allows for the appearance of 'Welsh' in the title, of
course, that full rhyme being too ludicrous had the 'belch' been
retained in the body of the poem. But let me continue to ponder this
title, and the 'lighter trance' arguments Graves might have mustered
to change it from 'Railway Carriage'. In his *Listener* interview with
Leslie Norris, he describes the origin of the poem:

> It started when my father and I were in a train compartment of the
> old Cambrian railway. The train was going round that curve from

Barmouth, through Lland-bedr, round into Harlech where you see the sea stretched out; and there was a policeman aboard, a Welsh policeman. He got very excited and started telling my father how he had recently seen a mermaid.

The report of a mermaid-sighting would have been dear to the heart of Alfred Perceval Graves (1846–1931), himself the author of so many poems having to do with 'queer things', particularly 'fairies and ghosts'. I think of 'The Fairy Host', a versification of a prose passage translated by Kuno Meyer from 'The Book of Leinster', with its representation of, yet again, a noisesome otherworldly troop:

> Pure white the shields their arms upbear,
> With silver emblems rare o'ercast;
> Amid blue glittering blades they go,
> The horns they blow are *loud of blast* ... [my emphasis]

These fairies are part of the little platoon sighted by William Allingham ('down along the rocky shore / some make their home'). More importantly in this instance, they have found their way out of a poem collected in Robert Louis Stevenson's *A Child's Garden of Verses* (1885):

> Faster than fairies, faster than witches,
> Bridges and houses, hedges and ditches.

The title of the Stevenson poem is, as you may recall, 'From a *Railway Carriage*' [my emphasis]. But that coincidence is just *one* reason why Graves is inclined to drop his first title. The main reason is connected to his relationship with his father. That this relationship was troubled is clear from the tone of Robert Graves's musings in *Goodbye to All That*:

I am glad in a way that my father was a poet. This at least saved me from any false reverence of poets, and his work was never an oppression to me. I am even very pleased when I meet people who know his work and not mine. Some of his songs I sing without prejudice; when washing up after meals or shelling peas or on similar occasions. He never once tried to teach me how to write, or showed any understanding of my serious work; he was always more ready to ask advice about his own work than to offer it for mine.

Goodbye to All That was published in 1929, and Robert Graves had to wait only a year to hear some 'advice' from his father in the form of Alfred Pervceval Graves's *To Return To All That*:

> In writing of [Robert] I must point out that there is much in his autobiography that I do not accept as accurate. For the change in his outlook I hold the war and recent experiences responsible. To these I impute his bitter and hasty criticism of people who never wished him harm ... He gives me no credit for the interest I always felt and showed in his poetry. During the War I offered poems of his to editor after editor, and even arranged with Harold Munro of the Poetry Book Shop, to whom I introduced Robert, for the publication of *Over the Brazier*.

A.P. Graves goes on to make much of the fact that, while serving as a Royal Welch Fusilier, Robert was wounded and reported dead in *The Times* of 3 August 1916.

> The first two doctors who had seen him had thought his case hopeless. The second of these, wanting his place in the clearing station for a more hopeful case, sent him off to the base hospital... He was still regarded as a hopeless case when he wrote his first letter home in the train.

And, then, A.P. Graves makes a throwaway remark which, like so many throwaway remarks, is bang on target:

> The journey to Rouen he has himself described as a nightmare, *and for some years after the war he was unable to go in any train without feeling violently sick* [my emphasis].

I want to propose that Graves's association of the 'Railway Carriage' with his trauma, his father, and his father's dismissal of him in *To Return To All That* (1930), are the main reasons for his changing the title of the poem in 1938. Let me focus on the trauma for the moment, and try to connect this with a key image from another poem from *Fairies and Fusiliers*. In 'Escape', Graves describes how, while he '*was* dead, an hour or more' [Graves's emphasis], he met Cerberus:

Cerberus stands and grins above me now,
Wearing three heads – lion, and lynx and sow.
'Quick, a revolver! But my Webley's gone,
Stolen! ... No bombs ... no knife ... The crowd swarms on,
Bellows, hurls stones ... Not even a honeyed sop ...
Nothing ... Good Cerberus! Good dog! ... But stop!
Stay! ... A great luminous thought ... I do believe
There's still some morphia that I bought on leave.'
Then swiftly Cerberus' wide mouths I cram
With army biscuit smeared with ration jam;
And sleep lurks in the luscious plum and apple.
He crunches, swallows, stiffens, seems to grapple
With the all-powerful poppy ... then a snore,
A crash; the beast blocks up the corridor
With monstrous hairy carcase, red and dun –
Too late! for I've sped through
                    O life! O sun!

The coloration of Cerberus ('red and dun') tallies with that of the
one conventionally coloured 'thing' in 'Welsh Incident' that 'was
puce / or perhaps more like *crimson*, but not *purplish*' [my emphasis].
The fact that one head of Cerberus is that of a 'sow' relates it to the
'grunting beast' of 'Letter to S.S.' and 'the most odd, indescribable
thing of all' that makes 'the very loud, respectable noise' in 'Welsh
Incident'. In *The White Goddess* (1948), Graves would describe how
Cerberus is one of those beasts likely to visit the poet while he or she
is in the ecstasy in which poems get made:

> To think with perfect clarity in a poetic sense one must first rid
> oneself of a great deal of intellectual encumbrance, including all
> dogmatic doctrinal prepossessions: membership of any political
> party or religious sect or literary school deforms the poetic sense –
> as it were, introduces something irrelevant and destructive into the
> magic circle, drawn with a rowan, hazel or willow rod, within which
> the poet insulates himself for the poetic act.

This is precisely the enclosed openness, if I may call it that, which

Graves encourages the scientist to cultivate in 'Nine Hundred Iron Chariots':

> He will see that the future of thought does not lie in the cosmical nonsense-region of electronic computers, but in the Paradisal region of what he will not be ashamed to call 'magic'.

In the case of 'Welsh Incident', however, Graves has allowed himself to introduce something 'irrelevant and destructive into the magic circle', namely his own 'intellectual encumbrance'. In an effort to make a point about 'respectability', he uses the word 'respectable' when the logic of the poem cries out for the word '*dis*respectable', perhaps even '*disrespectful*', which is surely how the Welsh congregation would perceive 'groaning to oneself on Easter morning'. As we've seen before, however, the poem survives the obstacles put in its way ('the beast [that] blocks up the corridor') and, like Graves surviving his near-death experience, like the Christ rising again from his 'sea-cave' at 'half-past three / On Easter Tuesday last', manages to 'sp[e]ed through' to the sun.

If poets named Graves are likely to be much exercised by 'ghosts', so a poet named Day-Lewis is likely to be exercised by 'the *day* of harvest' [my emphasis], a phrase we meet in the first line of the fifth stanza of 'A Failure'. Lest we think this far-fetched, we might remind ourselves that his autobiography of 1960 was entitled *The Buried* Day [my emphasis]. One of the main activities having to do with a 'day' is winning it, of course, winning being a word derived from, or cognate with, the Middle Low German *winnen*, meaning quite specifically 'to till the ground'. The imagery of 'A Failure' is deeply imbued with a sense of country lore. Though Cecil Day-Lewis, born in 1904 in Ballintubber, County Laois, moved to England when he was two years old, I like to think of that Irish landscape imprinting itself on him in the way that the landscape of County Monaghan imprinted itself on another Irish poet born in 1904:

Now leave the check-reins slack,
The seed is flying far today –
The seed like stars against the black
Eternity of April clay.

This seed is potent as the seed
Of knowledge in the Hebrew Book,
So drive your horses in the creed
Of God the Father as a stook.

Forget the men on Brady's hill.
Forget what Brady's boy may say.
For destiny will not fulfill
Unless you let the harrow play.

Forget the worm's opinion too
Of hooves and pointed harrow-pins,
For you are driving your horses through
The mist where Genesis begins.

Patrick Kavanagh's appeals to Genesis and allusions to Blake's
Proverbs of Hell ('the cut worm forgives the plough') give 'To the Man
after the Harrow' an oddly literary tinge, especially if read in the light
of Kavanagh's reputation for groundedness. Day-Lewis, meanwhile, is
no less *au courant* with the ins and outs of ploughing:

> The soil was deep and the field well-sited,
> The seed was sound.

By the time we get to the end of the second line, however, there's a
hint that this may not be a poem simply about ploughing. The word
'sound' may be read both in the sense of 'free from disease, infirmity,
or injury' and 'the particular auditory effect produced by a special
cause' (*OED*), such as the sound at the heart of music and poetry:

> The soil was deep and the field well-sited,
> The seed was sound.
> Average luck with the weather, one thought,
> And the crop would abound.

The imagery of the poem, however matter of fact, points to at least major literary influence. We might remember that 'A Failure' was included in *Poems 1943–1947* (1948), the first book of poems Day-Lewis published after his brilliant translations of Virgil's *The Georgics*.

> I've noticed seed long chosen and tested with utmost care
> Fall off, if each year the largest
> Be not hand-picked by human toil. For a law of nature
> Makes all things go to the bad, lose ground and fall away.

But Day-Lewis goes beyond Virgil (Book I, lines 197–200) in presenting a metaphorical landscape, one that his readers would have recognised from at least as far back as the title poem of the 1931 collection *From Feathers to Iron*, in which the coming to term of a child is compared to a crop coming to fruition. Here we find lines such as 'Twenty weeks near past / Since the seed took to earth' and 'Beautiful brood the cornlands, and you are heavy; / Leafy the boughs – they also hide big fruit'. In 1931, Day-Lewis had been just as much exercised by the social ramifications of bringing another child into the world:

> What were we at, the moment when we kissed –
> Extending the franchise
> To an indifferent class, would we enlist
> Fresh power who know not how to be so great?
> Beget and breed a life – what's this
> But to perpetuate
> Man's labour, to enlarge a rank estate?

Day-Lewis is appealing here in 'From Feathers to Iron' to a central tenet of Karl Marx and Friedrich Engels, the latter of whom, in the *The Origin of the Family, Private Property and the State* (1884), identified the domestication of plants and animals as the beginning of organised labour. While he may be having a little fun with the double sense of 'labour', meaning both 'physical exertion directed to the supply of the material wants of the community' and 'the pains and efforts of childbirth', Day-Lewis is most interested in making a point to do with the 'the general body of labourers and operatives, viewed in its relation to the body of capitalists, or with regard to its political interests and claims' (*OED*):

> Planted out here some virtue still may flower,
> But our dead follies too –
> A shock of buried weeds to turn it sour.
> Draw up conditions – will the heir conform?
> Or thank us for the favour, who
> Inherits a bankrupt firm,
> Worn-out machinery, an exhausted farm.

By the time Day-Lewis returns to this system of imagery in 'A Failure', there is more than a faint sense that the 'bankrupt', the 'worn-out' and the 'exhausted' are terms applicable to the political agenda that had preoccupied his earlier self and which might now seem overly restrictive. The word 'abound' at the end of the fourth line prepares the ground, as it were, for the notion of containment it (somewhat paradoxically) contains. The idea of a boundary is also included in the phrase 'headland to headland' in the fourth stanza, since part of the *OED* definition of 'headland' is 'a strip of land in a ploughed field, left for convenience in turning the plough at the end of the furrows, or near the border; in old times used as a *boundary*' [my emphasis]. The 'failure', though, of this poem has less to do with political matters than literary – the work of art that, despite tending, comes to nothing. These 'headland' strictures of Day-Lewis's poem also have literary antecedents, deriving partly from the 1942 poem by Day-Lewis's strict contemporary, Patrick Kavanagh:

> A dog lying on a torn jacket under a heeled-up cart,
> A horse nosing along the posied *headland*, trailing
> A rusty plough [my emphasis].

This section of 'The Great Hunger' ends with an eroticised description: 'Where men are spanging across wide furrows, / Lost in the passion that never needs a wife – / The pricks that pricked were the pointed pins of harrows.'

It seems that it's the mechanism of a harrow rather than a plough to which Day-Lewis appeals at the end of 'A Failure':

> But it's useless to argue the why and wherefore.
>   When the crop is so thin,
> There's nothing to do but to set the teeth
>   And plough it in.

In this instance, the word 'plough' may be read metaphorically. The
other way of reading it is literally, of course, and reading the phrase
'to set the teeth' metaphorically, as though it were an amalgam of
'to set one's face' and 'to grin and bear it', along with the slightly
unfortunate resonances of 'to set one's teeth on edge'. There is
resignation here before the turn of the wheel of Fortune, the goddess
whose *'fortunate* acres / Seemed solid gold' [my emphasis]. The
fortunatus comes directly from Book 2, lines 458–500, of *The Georgics*:

> Oh, too lucky for words, if only he knew his luck,
> Is the countryman who far from the clash of armaments
> Lives, and rewarding earth is lavish of all he needs!

The idea of 'fortune' implies the existence of a system beyond
oneself, be it the cycle of the seasons, the endless round of growth
and decay and re-growth, or some notion of poetic inspiration. In
The Lyric Impulse, the book based on his 1964–65 Norton lectures at
Harvard, Day-Lewis describes poetry as a 'gift from the goddess'. He
goes on to describe what is essentially a Gravesian relationship
between poet and goddess:

> The Muse, though she visit her poet but fitfully, is the ground of his
> being. She will not come meekly to his call; but when she does
> come, she possesses him entire, and her absence leaves a void which
> cannot be filled with other preoccupations. He may have no
> religious belief, may even feel no need for god, yet he is religious in
> the sense that he cannot live by material values; though he may not
> know it, he is the man in Browning's poem – the one 'Through a
> whole campaign of the world's life and death, / Doing the King's
> work all the dim day long'.

The 'King' in question is from Browning's 'How It Strikes a
Contemporary', and is to be thought of partly as 'our Lord the King'

in the Christian world-picture. The description of him continues:

> In his old coat and up to knees in mud,
> Smoked like a herring, dining on a crust, –
> And, now the day is won, relieved at once.

That phrase 'now the day is won' would, yet again, have had a
resonance (conscious or unconscious) for Day-Lewis, and it may
account for the possibility of the poetic unconscious in the phrase
'though he may not know it'. For the 'King' in 'How It Strikes a
Contemporary' is also a poet, specifically a version of Shelley, and
the poem was written at about the same time as Browning's
'Introductory Essay to the *Letters of Percy Bysshe Shelley*' (1852). It's
in that essay, we may recall, that Browning makes his famous
distinction between the objective and subjective poet. The latter is
'rather a seer ... than a fashioner, and what he produces will be less
a work than an effluence'. Now, according to Browning, the
'subjective' poet is particularly likely to fail, and is described in terms
which Day-Lewis seems to have taken over not only in *The Lyric
Impulse* but also in 'A Failure':

> Although of such depths of *failure* [my emphasis] there can be no
> question here, we must in every case betake ourselves to the review
> of a poet's life ere we determine some of the nicer questions
> concerning his poetry, – more especially if the performance we seek
> to estimate aright has been obstructed and cut short of completion
> by circumstances, – a disastrous youth or a premature death. We
> may learn from the biography whether his spirit invariably saw and
> spoke from the last height to which it had attained. An absolute
> vision is not for this world, but we are permitted a continual
> approximation to it, every degree of which in the individual,
> provided it exceed the attainment of the masses, must procure him
> a clear advantage. Did the poet ever attain to a higher platform
> than where he rested and exhibited a result? Did he know more
> than he spoke of?

The concerns of the speaker of 'A Failure' are remarkably of a piece
with Browning's here, 'perhaps his own high hopes had made / The
wizened look tall' echoing the imagery of Browning's 'clear

advantage', but it's useful to argue the why and wherefore, echoing Browning's 'an absolute vision is not for this world'. The notion that a poet might 'know more than he spoke of' is connected, I think, with the idea that the poem (the 'effluence' for which the poet is a gutter) might 'know more' than the poet. It's when the poet recognises that his or her field is 'wan and weedy' rather than showing the 'solid ground' to which it aspires that he or she is forced to counter vision with revision. At that point the poet is coming under the scrutiny of the poem, and may or may not be able to look it straight in the eyes. This is precisely the relationship subsequent readers will have with the poem – subsequent readers who may be better able for, may bring more to bear on, the poem than the first writer.

If one of a poem's main aims is to continue to present itself as a problem only it has raised, a poem gladly enlists other readers in order to further itself, in order to find the equivalent of a 'gutter' for its 'copious blood', a 'black divide' in which writer/reader and reader/writer lie down together.

Like the speakers of 'Welsh Incident' and 'A Failure', the speaker of 'Keeping Going', a speaker who is fairly coterminous with the historical figure of Seamus Heaney, is as much engaged by artistic dilemmas and deliverances as by Hugh Heaney's 'shout[s]' and 'laugh[s] above the revs'. Those 'revs', or 'revolutions', represent one form of 'turn' against which the poet, and his brother, display resolution. The other 'turn' is the 'attack of illness, faintness, or the like' (*OED*) from which Hugh recovers towards the end of the poem.

'Keeping Going' was collected in *The Spirit Level* (1996) and is one of a number of poems in that volume which are dedicated to friends and family of the poet. The dedication 'for Hugh' is reminiscent of a dedication we saw three poems earlier in 'A Brigid's Girdle', which is 'for Adele'. Just as 'Hugh' is addressed overtly in the body of the poem as 'my dear brother', the 'Adele' in question is named covertly, in the body of 'A Brigid's Girdle', in the lines:

> I heard the mocking bird
> And a delicious, articulate
>
> Flight of small plinkings from a dulcimer
> Like feminine rhymes migrating to the north
> Where you faced the music and the ache of summer
> And earth's foreknowledge gathered in the earth.

The 'feminine rhyme' on 'dulcimer' is 'Dalsimer', the full name of Adele Dalsimer, a scholar and co-founder of the Irish Studies Program at Boston College, who would die from multiple myeloma in 2000. 'A Brigid's Girdle' closes with the 'revolutionary' image of 'the motions you go through going through the thing', which connects the poem thematically with 'Keeping *Going*' [my emphasis]. That 'dulcimer' also connects the poems, given that the most famous dulcimer, accompanied by damsel, is to be found in Samuel Taylor Coleridge's 'Kubla Khan', the archetypical 'trance' document, at least according to Coleridge.

'A Brigid's Girdle' connects with 'Keeping Going' in another, even more subliminal, way. Brigid is a version of a bear-goddess who is associated with fertility and her feast day, 1 February, corresponds to the Celtic festival of Imbolc, which as Seamas Ó Cathain tells us in *The Festival of Brigit* (1995), his great study of the bear-goddess, is 'a word whose basic meaning has much to do with the notion of milking and milk-production'. The positioning of Hugh Heaney 'in the milking parlour … between two cows' is no accident. There is a distinct aural association between Ó hAoine, the Irish version of Heaney's name, and *aonaigh*, the genitive of the word *aonach*, 'a fair'. Indeed, Hugh Heaney is continuing in the tradition of cattle-dealing espoused by his and the poet's father, Patrick, whose spirit appears in 'The Strand':

> The dotted line my father's ashplant made
> On Sandymount Strand
> Is something else the tide won't wash away.

This three-line poem, also from *The Spirit Level*, is terrifically resonant. The title refers not only to a strand in the sense of 'the land bordering the sea' but the transferred sense of strand as 'a thread or filament' as in 'strands of thought' (*OED*). Interwoven rather neatly here are the figures of James Joyce (with his trademark drover's ashplant) on Sandymount Strand and the drover father of the poet whose house overlooks Sandymount Strand. The 'sand' is a significant element in the Ó hAoine iconography since it's still believed in some quarters that sand taken from the grave of the twelfth-century Saint Murrough O'Heaney brings luck, though only if it's 'lifted' by a Heaney descendant. Murrough O'Heaney's grave is in Banagher, County Derry, and it just happens that the third-to-last poem in *The Spirit Level* is entitled 'At Banagher' and concerns 'a journeyman tailor who was my antecedent'.

The 'strand' by which Heaney connects to his literary antecedent, James Joyce, is two-ply. The second ply is summoned up by the word 'wash' in 'something else the tide won't wash away', a word which connects it to the process of white*wash*ing that is described so vividly in 'Keeping Going':

> But the slop of the actual job
> Of brushing walls, the watery grey
> Being lashed on in broad swatches, then drying out
> Whiter and whiter, all that worked like magic.

The description of the process of whitewashing chimes with the description of Joyce's method of composition as described so memorably by A. Walton Litz in *The Art of James Joyce*, where he writes of *Work in Progress*:

> Usually the basic outline of a paragraph remained the same throughout its growth. Joyce seems to have thought of his original units as fundamental designs which could be expanded indefinitely through his techniques of amplification.

The process of whitewashing might well be described as a 'technique of amplification', or 'an elaboration of a basic text', as Litz also puts it. Litz quotes Herbert Read's observation that 'the closest analogy to the literary method of *Work in Progress* is perhaps to be found in the early graphic art of Joyce's own country, the abstract involved ornament of the Celts'. In the way that Joyce incorporated a reference to the 'Tunc' page of 'The Book of Kells' in the passage about 'pidgin fella Balkelly' who 'augmentationed himself in caloripeia to vision so throughsighty' and achieved the condition of 'pure hueglut', Heaney's description of the 'grey lashed on in broad swatches' that becomes its own 'hueglut' is a brilliant description of the poem's own method of achieving brilliance. What works 'like magic' in the poem is the visual artist's technique involving successive 'broad thin layer[s] of colour laid on by a continuous movement of the brush' (OED).

There is indeed a magical quality to the layering of the narratives of make-believe 'piper's sporrans', the all-too-believable fate of the 'part-time reservist' who leaves 'a clean spot where his head had been' and 'the actual job / of brushing walls'. All bleed together until, like Hugh, we can't be certain if we should call a whitewash brush a piper's sporran or 'the piper's sporrans whitewash brushes'. Similarly, in the poem 'Widgeon' (Station Island, 1984) there's some confusion about the source of the 'small widgeon cries' that seem to be emitted by the man who 'found, he says, the voice box' of the duck. This 'Widgeon' is casting its voice, almost inaudibly this time, through 'Keeping Going', resonant in that sense of the term 'whitewash' meaning 'to cover up, conceal, or gloss over the faults or blemishes of'. I'm thinking of the near version of widgeon to be found in the name Widgery, the controversial Lord Chief Justice whose report on the events of 'Bloody Sunday' in Derry in 1972 was famously described by John Hume, the SDLP Member of Parliament, as 'whitewash'. The figure of John Hume, I propose, is another ghostly presence in 'Keeping Going', since Heaney and Hume were contemporaries at St Columb's College in Derry, the school in which Heaney first came upon 'that scene, with Macbeth helpless and desperate / In his nightmare'.

In his most recent collection, Electric Light (2001), Heaney gives us 'The Real Names' of at least some of his fellow students who took part in these school productions and, in one passage, connects a scene from Macbeth with a scene of violent action from the 1950s:

Duncan's horses, plastered in wet, surge up
Wild as the chestnut tree one terrible night
In Mossbawn, the aerial rod like a mast
Whiplashed in tempest, my mother rocking and oching
And blessing herself –
                              the breach in nature open
As the back of the raiders' lorry hammering on
For the Monaghan border, blood loosed in a scrim
From the tailboard, the volunteer screaming *O Jesus!*
O merciful Jesus.

The burden of these lines might be said to be that there's no
delineation between art and history. The very thing that would
mediate between the two, the 'scrim', or 'open-weave muslin or
hessian fabric used in ... the theatre to create the illusion of a solid
wall or to suggest haziness, etc., according to the lighting' (*Collins
English Dictionary*), is composed of 'blood', just as it's the 'smoky hair'
in 'Keeping Going' which engages in its own stagecraft in '*curtaining
a cheek*' [my emphasis]. The graphic description of the wounded IRA
man in the back of the lorry is reminiscent of the graphic description
of the dead 'reservist' in 'Keeping Going' who 'saw an ordinary face /
for what it was' and the dead shopkeeper from the poem 'Station
Island', whose murderers were 'barefaced as they would be in the day,
/ shites thinking they were the be-all and the end-all' (*Station Island*,
1984).

The 'nightmare' in which Macbeth is 'helpless and desperate' is
also the 'nightmare from which I am trying to awake', as Stephen
Dedalus describes 'history' (Irish history, to be precise), in *Ulysses*
(1922). This occurs in the 'Nestor' chapter of the novel, where much
is made of Stephen being seen as a 'bullockbefriending bard' who's
entrusted with Mr Deasy's letter on 'foot and mouth disease' in cattle.
The other great 'nightmare' in the hinterland of *Ulysses* involves
Oliver St John Gogarty's fellow Oxford student and Martello Tower
dweller, Samuel Chenevix (later Dermot) Trench, as Richard
Ellmann explains in his *James Joyce*:

> What happened was that during the night of September 14 (1904)
> Trench began to scream in his sleep. He was convinced that a black

panther was about to spring. Half waking, he snatched his revolver and shot at the fireplace beside which Joyce was sleeping. After having dispatched his prey, he turned back to sleep. While Joyce trembled, Gogarty seized the gun. Then Trench, again ridden by nightmare, screamed and reached again for his revolver. Gogarty called out, 'Leave him to me', and shot not the panther but some pans hanging above Joyce's bed, which tumbled down on the recumbent poet. The terrified Joyce considered this fusillade his dismissal; without a word he dressed and left, having – at that hour – to walk all the way to Dublin.

This episode ghosts 'Keeping Going' in an almost invisible way, in that 'freshly-opened, pungent, reeking *trench*' [my emphasis], and its near version, the 'gutter' that's fed with 'copious blood'. This blood, like the 'matte tacky blood / on the bricklayer's knuckles, like the damson stain / that seeped through his packed lunch' in 'Damson', another piece from *The Spirit Level*, is associated with a heraldic moment. The word 'gules', indeed, is the first word of 'Damson', signifying 'red, as one of the heraldic colours' (OED). In 'Keeping Going', the elaborate positioning of the 'reservist' guardant, 'a gun in his own face', on a field of argent confirms a tendency for the humdrum to become heraldic in a way beloved of Joyce. Now, Joyce and his ashplant, with which the character of Stephen is associated from the outset of *Ulysses*, informs 'Keeping Going' in at least one further, rather more important, way. We first met Heaney meeting Joyce in *Station Island*, in the title poem of which, we remember, the speaker meets 'a tall man' who 'walked straight as a rush / upon his ashplant' and who argues that 'you lose more of yourself than you redeem / doing the decent thing'.

I want to end my discussion of 'Keeping Going' with an observation or two on this 'trench' in which Heaney has been at war with himself for so long, a muddy ground out of which have come some of his very best poems, including this one. It's the area presided over by what we might call, to pun on one of his titles, 'The *Gutter*al Muse' [my emphasis], in which Heaney finds himself 'between two cows' – one representing the urge toward an Arnoldian 'adequacy', perhaps even an Arnoldian 'deliverance', and the position we saw earlier espoused by Joyce in 'Station Island':

'The English language
belongs to us. You are raking at dead fires,

rehearsing the old whinges at your age.
That subject people stuff is a cod's game,
infantile, like this peasant pilgrimage.

You lose more of yourself than you redeem
doing the decent thing.'

The impulse towards redemption is very understandable, but even
more understandable is the recognition that, as the speaker has it in
the shopkeeper section of 'Station Island', there is no 'buying back'
when it comes to those 'shites thinking they were the be-all and end-
all':

'Not that it is any *consolation* [my emphasis]
but they were caught,' I told him, 'and got jail.'

Allied to the ideas of redemption and consolation is the idea of
'restoration', an idea we meet in the second section of 'Keeping
Going':

Where had we come from, what was this kingdom
We knew we'd been restored to?

This 'kingdom' is only partly the realm of Browning's 'our lord the
King' in what I described above as 'the Christian world-picture'. Like
Browning's character in 'How It Strikes a Contemporary', the king is
also an artist, the kingdom one we enter by the 'magic' of the art of
whitewashing. One of the poignancies of 'Keeping Going' is the
speaker's assertion – one we don't expect from a Heaney speaker –
that, despite the 'magic' of Hugh's calling 'the piper's sporrans
whitewash brushes', there's the insurmountable fact of the limitations
of art:

But you cannot make the dead walk or right wrong.

This is not to say that a poem, such as any of the three we looked
at today, doesn't have *some* efficacy in the world, doesn't effect *some*

change. It must change something, as the three examples I've looked at in this lecture so elegantly demonstrate. One of the ways in which they do so is to clear their own space, bringing us 'all together there in a foretime', if I may borrow that phrase from the third section of 'Keeping Going'. This 'foretime' is the 'kingdom' to which we are to be restored, of course, a sense of 'foreknowledge' that Heaney associates with a work of art in 'Poet's Chair' in *The Spirit Level*. This condition of a 'foretime' of the poem is, yet again, a version of what I described earlier as the 'problem' to which the poem is a 'solution'. We appeal to the 'foretime' of 'Welsh Incident' and recognise that, despite the wobble on 'respectable', the poem triumphs over the person through whom it was written. We appeal to the 'foretime' of 'A Failure' and recognise that it meets its own 'solid gold' standard, winning its own day. We appeal to the 'foretime' of 'Keeping Going' and recognise, as we emerge with Hugh from our 'turn', that to carry itself forward in the world – testing itself, and us, against a sense of how it itself 'was / In the beginning, is now and shall be' – *is* indeed the end of the poem.

Notes on Contributors

MAUREEN BOYLE grew up in County Tyrone. While still at school she won an UNESCO medal for a book of poetry commemorating *The Year of the Child*. Her first 'adult' poem won second prize in the Dun Laoghaire International Poetry Competition in 2002. She was the runner-up in the Patrick Kavanagh Awards in 2004. A teacher, broadcaster, bookseller and freelance writer, she is currently working on her first collection of poems.

MIRIAM DE BÚRCA was born in Germany and raised in Ireland. An artist and filmmaker living and working in Belfast, she has a BA in Drawing and Painting from the Glasgow School of Art and completed a Masters in Fine Art with distinction at the University of Ulster in 2000. The upside-down-tree appears courtesy of the artist and was first published in 2004 on the cover of a Festschrift for Miriam's father, Eoin Bourke, Professor Emeritus of German at NUI Galway.

NORMAN THOMAS DI GIOVANNI co-authored Jorge Luis Borges's autobiography in English and has translated sixteen of his books. Di Giovanni's essays on Borges, *The Lesson of the Master*, appeared in 2003.

THEO DORGAN'S most recent book, *Songs of Earth and Light*, was published as part of the Cork 2005 European Capital of Culture programme and features translations of the Slovene poet, Barbara Korun. *Sailing for Home*, a prose work about a transatlantic journey, was published by Penguin Ireland in 2004.

JOHN WILSON FOSTER is currently a Leverhulme Professor to the United Kingdom, attached to the Academy for Irish Cultural Heritages at the University of Ulster. His recent books include *Recoveries: Neglected Episodes in Irish Cultural History 1860–1912* (2002); *The Age of Titanic: Cross-Currents in Anglo-American Culture* (2002); *Titanic* (1999); and (as senior editor) *Nature in Ireland: A Scientific and Cultural History* (1997).

ALAN GILLIS lectures in English at the University of Ulster at Coleraine. He is the author of *Irish Poetry of the 1930s* (2005) and co-editor, with Aaron Kelly, of *Critical Ireland: New Essays on Literature and Culture* (2001). His first collection of poetry, *Somebody, Somewhere* (2004), was shortlisted for the *Irish Times* Poetry Now Award and won the 2005 Rupert and Eithne Strong Award.

SEAMUS HEANEY is a Foreign Member of the American Academy of Arts and Letters and held the chair of Professor of Poetry at Oxford from 1989 to 1994. In 1995 he received the Nobel Prize in Literature. Based in Dublin, he spends part of the year in the United States, where he is Boylston Professor of Rhetoric and Oratory at the University of Harvard.

EDNA LONGLEY is the author of numerous books including *The Living Stream: Literature and Revisionism in Ireland* (1994) and *Poetry and Posterity* (2001).

In 2001 she also edited *The Bloodaxe Book of Twentieth-Century Poetry from Britain and Ireland* (2001). She is currently Professor Emerita at Queen's University, based in the Seamus Heaney Centre for Poetry.

CATHAL McCABE was born in Newry in 1963. A graduate of the universities of York and Oxford, he lived in Poland for some fourteen years, working as a lecturer at the University of Łódź and as Literature Consultant with the British Council in Warsaw. In 2003 he was appointed Director of the Irish Writers' Centre in Dublin. His poems have been published in numerous periodicals and anthologies including *New Writing 7* (1998) and *The New Irish Poets* (2004). His first (unpublished) collection was awarded the 2004 Rupert and Eithne Strong Award for Poetry.

MEDBH McGUCKIAN is the author of eleven collections of poetry, the most recent being *The Book of the Angel* (2004). She has received numerous awards including the Rooney Prize for Irish Literature (1982), the Alice Hunt Bartlett Award (1983) and the Cheltenham Prize (1989). In 2002 she won the Forward Prize for Best Single Poem. She is currently a Creative Writing Fellow at the Seamus Heaney Centre for Poetry.

PAUL MULDOON is a Fellow of the Royal Society of Literature and the American Academy of Arts and Sciences. Among the many honours he has received are the T.S. Eliot Prize (1994), the *Irish Times* Poetry Prize (1997), the Griffin International Prize for Excellence in Poetry (2003), the American Ireland Fund Literary Award (2004) and the Shakespeare Prize (2004). *Moy Sand and Gravel* (2003) won the 2003 Pulitzer Prize. He is Professor in the Humanities at Princeton University.

DAVID WHEATLEY has published two collections of poetry, *Thirst* (1997) and *Misery Hill* (2000), and co-authored a third, *Three Legged Dog* (2003) with Caitríona O'Reilly. He is co-founder, with Justin Quinn, of *Metre* magazine, and has edited a selection of the poetry of James Clarence Mangan for Gallery Press (2003). He lectures in English at the University of Hull.